WARRIOR COMPASSION

WARRIOR COMPASSION

UNLEASHING THE HEALING POWER OF MEN

SEAN HARVEY

MANUSCRIPTS
PRESS

WARRIOR COMPASSION
Unleashing the Healing Power of Men

ISBN   979-8-88926-796-6 *Paperback*

979-8-88926-797-3 *Ebook*

Warrior Compassion is dedicated to men around the world. Men who yearn for deeper connection, intimacy, and love in their lives. Men who seek to break down the walls of disconnection, isolation, and loneliness. Men trying to make sense of a world that is rapidly changing around them. Men who feel lost, confused, or frustrated as they are being told they must change because they are broken. Men who feel left out and unsure how they fit in the world or where they belong. Men who suffer in silence from deep wounding and seek healing at a soul level. This book offers a roadmap for men's soul healing as a catalyst for systems change—the type of healing that liberates men to live their truth, love differently, and make a meaningful difference in the world.

Imagine What's Possible

"Imagine what's possible in the world when we come into our integrated selves, where we see each other in our full humanity and possess deeper levels of compassion for ourselves and everyone around us."

—SEAN HARVEY, CHIEF COMPASSION OFFICER AND FOUNDER, WARRIOR COMPASSION MEN'S STUDIO

CONTENTS

INTRODUCTION   1

PART I.   **THE WOUNDING AND HEALING OF MEN**   **7**

CHAPTER 1.   THE PLIGHT OF THE WOUNDED WARRIOR   11

CHAPTER 2.   WARRIOR COMPASSION AS A HEALING
              POWER   21

PART II.   **UNPACKING MY HEALING JOURNEY**   **33**

CHAPTER 3.   MY HEALING JOURNEY AT EILEEN FISHER   37

CHAPTER 4.   EMBARKING ON MY SOUL ADVENTURE   55

PART III.   **UNLOCKING THE HEALING**   **65**

CHAPTER 5.   PREPARE FOR YOUR HEALING JOURNEY   69

CHAPTER 6.   BEGIN THE JOURNEY AS AN INQUIRY   83

CHAPTER 7.   DEEPEN SPIRITUAL UNDERSTANDING   95

PART IV.   **UNBLOCKING THE WOUNDS**   **107**

CHAPTER 8.   UNEARTH THE DEEPER WOUNDS   111

CHAPTER 9.   EMBRACE THE SOUL-HEALING JOURNEY   123

CHAPTER 10. WALK THE SOUL-HEALING PATH   131

CHAPTER 11. EXPAND YOUR CAPACITY TO LOVE   157

PART V.   UNLEASHING THE HEALING POWER   171

CHAPTER 12. EMERGE AS A HEALING WARRIOR   175

CHAPTER 13. DISCOVER YOUR SOUL'S MISSION   183

CHAPTER 14. LEAD WITH WARRIOR COMPASSION   195

CHAPTER 15. UNLEASH YOUR HEALING POWER IN
             THE WORLD   213

ACKNOWLEDGMENTS   219

APPENDIX   223

ABOUT THE AUTHOR   229

INTRODUCTION

———

"Keep Your Powder Dry"

My father and I didn't always have the best relationship. My dad was a second-generation long-haul truck driver and had been on the road for over forty-three years (a boat hauler for most of those years). He was also a Vietnam veteran, Jehovah's Witness, and a Republican. I'm a former college professor who left a consulting career on Wall Street, went on my healing journey while working for a fashion company, became an interfaith minister, and now works to deepen compassion among police officers and military personnel. We didn't always see eye to eye, but I always loved and respected him despite our differences.

Growing up, my father was on the road often, so I typically saw him at home for about a weekend every three or four months. From about three years old, I would go on the road with my pops for long weekends or summers. I often say I learned about masculinity and what it means to be a man in truck stops.

He was a wise and complex man. While he didn't go to college, he often said he got his education from the school of hard knocks. I still remember riding in the truck with him as he smoked his cigar and listening to him share his thoughts. He would randomly drop some serious wisdom, and I would sit there in total awe. He'd usually talk about what it takes to be a quality gentleman and a God-fearing man. He'd also share his reflections about how people treat each other in the world and how to treat people, especially women, with respect and kindness.

At the same time, he could also go into a silent rage from zero to sixty, and he knew it, as he used the CB handle "The Door Slammer." I remember when he threw my mom through a closet door because she didn't make dinner the right way. On another occasion, he spanked me when I was about three years old. As my mom tells it, I hit the wall from the spanking. Later that night, he told her that she would handle all punishments from now on. Otherwise, he was afraid he would probably kill me. As I said, he was a very complex man with his own demons.

Dad and Mom divorced when I was seven, and our relationship became even more distant. I came out as gay at sixteen to everyone but Dad, whom I told at twenty-seven. After I told him, we didn't speak or see each other again for another fourteen years. When we reconnected, I was told he was dying of thyroid cancer by my stepsister, but he couldn't do chemotherapy because he had a quadruple bypass, and his heart wasn't strong enough for it. So, he was just waiting to die.

I flew to Detroit with Matthew, my domestic partner of seven years at the time, to reconnect with my dad and his wife. It was honestly one of the most awkward reunions ever. My father apprehensively shook my hand that first day and told stories for the next five hours without asking one question. I suspected he was too afraid to get to know me or learn anything about my life. It was an excruciating weekend overall.

Later that week, when I was back in NYC, my dad called me and told me he didn't condone my life choice and I was going to hell. But he thought Matthew was a solid guy. With that said, the door had been open to reconnect, and Dad began to call me about once a month.

While I was initially reluctant, he was persistent (or stubborn, however you want to look at it) and continued to call and try to rebuild our relationship. This stubborn thing is something we had in common, and as he would often say, "Boy, you come by it naturally. Don't fight it." At a certain point, I told myself I had a choice: I could hold onto the resentment or lean into love and learn to forgive. I chose the latter.

As we began to talk about once a month, it took some time to get comfortable with each other. But with each call, it became a little easier. I remember one time when he was talking smack about politics, and I just began to challenge him, you know, with facts and stuff. At a certain point, he just started to laugh.

I said, "Wait. No one ever challenges you on your bullshit, do they?"

He laughed and said, "No."

I replied, "You know I'm your son, right? So, whatever you throw at me, I'm going to throw back harder and better. That's how the father-and-son thing works."

He laughed and said, "Yeah, I'm getting that."

We both realized at that moment we were legitimately father and son, even if, on many levels, we were worlds apart.

This was a turning point when we started to get each other. I was no longer his gay son, but just his son.

I began to embrace my dad with unconditional love and became more curious about his life. We continued opening up to each other. I told him my dreams, pain, stories from my past, and the big milestones in my life. He told me stories of his long hauls, favorite boats, cats, grandkids from this third marriage, and camping. Man, did he love to go camping and canoeing! It might be where my love of whitewater came from.

As we became closer, I asked him why he walked out on us when I was seven. He said, "Son, your mama started going to college. She started having these ideas, and she started to think for herself. I couldn't handle it, so I left. I never meant to hurt you, but I couldn't stay married to her." He wasn't holding back, and I just sat there dumbfounded by his honesty and reasons. At the same time, I appreciated that he was open and vulnerable enough to tell me the truth.

The weekend before he died, I drove from New York City to Detroit to visit him one last time. I wanted to experience his life as a trucker on some level, so I decided to make the drive. When I arrived at his bedside, I asked, "How did you drive a truck for forty-three years? I couldn't take the drive after nine hours." We spent the next twelve hours together, with Dad telling me stories about interstates, his travels, boats, and me busting his chops.

During the weekend, I asked my dad, "So, what advice would you give your only child, your only son?"

He said, "Son, keep your powder dry."

I asked, "My powder?"

He replied, "Your gunpowder, son, your gunpowder. Don't let anyone extinguish your flame. Be proud of who and what you are, and don't let anyone diminish who and what you are. I'm sorry for the pain I caused you over the years and that I wasn't there for you growing up. A day didn't go by when I didn't think about you, and I have always loved you and am proud of the man you've become."

I sat there stunned and in tears as I thought about the twists and turns in our relationship over the years. An hour later, during that visit, Dad asked me to feed him as he wasn't strong enough to lift his arms. I fed him applesauce with the greatest care, and in that instance, I got it. I viscerally felt unconditional love like I'd never experienced before. I remember thinking, *Oh, this is what love feels like.*

I left my father that weekend, truly forgiving him for the past. At the same time, he showed that he accepted me for the man I had become. Driving back from Detroit, I remember thinking my forgiveness allowed him to die in peace, and his acceptance permitted me to begin living my life fully. The father/son relationship can be quite tricky and complex. Healing the relationships with our fathers is one of the key steps in the healing journey for men.

As I reflect on the saying, "Keep your powder dry," I'm struck by the simplicity and wisdom of it. Although the origin of this phrase is unclear, it is commonly associated with military culture and tactics. In the past, gunpowder was an essential resource for soldiers, and its effectiveness greatly diminished if it became damp. Soldiers were therefore encouraged to take great care in storing and protecting their gunpowder and to avoid allowing external forces to compromise its effectiveness (Safire 1997).

In a broader sense, this saying suggests that one should not allow external forces to compromise their abilities or objectives. It also emphasizes the importance of maintaining one's values and principles in the face of external influences. Overall, this saying is a powerful reminder of the importance of staying focused, staying true to one's values and deeply held beliefs, and protecting one's resources. While its origins may be uncertain, the message behind the phrase is timeless and applicable in many contexts.

This phrase speaks to the essence of *Warrior Compassion*. This book offers a roadmap of inquiry for healing in a world where men, especially white straight men, are told they must change because something is broken, and many interpret that they are broken. This book is written to offer men inspiration and a sense of hope. It introduces a path to heal, rather than fix, by sharing insights, wisdom, and most importantly, questions. Questions each man can ask himself to discover his truth. At the heart of *Warrior Compassion* is a soul-healing journey for men steeped in the transforming power of unconditional love.

I have heard throughout my life that you can't love someone else until you learn to love yourself. And my response has always been the same: "But how do you do that?" Where's the roadmap to learn how to love? *Warrior Compassion* is written to share stories that inspire men as they discover new ways to love, the healing power that can transform the world. And this concept of warrior compassion can be defined as the self-love we can offer ourselves on our healing journeys.

I offer the saying to all men reading this book: "Keep your powder dry." As you look at yourself through a new lens and continue reading, take the time to honor and embrace your journey and allow your truth to reveal itself.

PART I

THE WOUNDING AND HEALING OF MEN

———

Lost in the Wilderness

A Prayer for the Wounded Warriors of the World

—SEAN HARVEY, INTERFAITH AND
INTERSPIRITUAL MINISTER

Lost are thee who roam aimlessly.
Lost are thee who have lost everything.
Lost are thee who yearn for belonging.
Lost are thee who have fallen to their knees.

Divine Spirit, we ask that you watch over the souls of
   these men.
Please shine your light through the wilderness to
   illuminate a new path.
Bring them comfort as they march forward, one step
   at a time.

Introduce their angels along the path so they can find
   deep roots.
Awakening their spirits to form a sacred compass.
Give them hope in their darkest hours and the courage
   to persevere.

When they are hopeless, send them a lifeline.
When they are lonely, send them a friend.
When they are hungry, send them a meal.
When they are lost, send them your light.

CHAPTER 1

THE PLIGHT OF THE WOUNDED WARRIOR

———

After another mass shooting in the US, this time in Uvalde, Texas, I sat on a virtual conference call with my Project Compassion team and US Senate staffers on the Judiciary Committee. Our thirty-minute conversation revolved around men's mental health, mass shootings, police shootings, and police and veteran suicides. As I listened to the way Democrats and Republicans were coming together—a rarity in 2022, where political division grew ever more apparent—to address the mass shooting and suicide epidemics in the US in a more bipartisan way, I realized I was sitting in one of the defining conversations of our time.

While mass shootings and suicides reflect a relatively small percentage of men, I want to talk openly about the plight of wounded warriors that reflect the challenges many men face. Most men today are confronted with societal expectations and pressures that demand them to be strong, stoic, and invulnerable. These cultural norms often discourage men from expressing their emotions and seeking help when needed, resulting in a significant emotional burden. The suppression of emotions can lead to many challenges, including depression, anxiety, addiction, and relationship difficulties.

Today, men suffering in silence is a stark reality, perpetuating many men's deep wounds and emotional struggles, hindering their well-being, and preventing them from receiving the support they need. It is time to break this cycle of silent suffering and create a culture that encourages open dialogue, empathy, and compassion for men's mental and emotional health. By addressing the plight of men suffering in silence, we can pave the way for healing, growth, and a more compassionate society that supports the well-being of all individuals, regardless of gender.

Many men carry deep emotional wounds behind the facade of strength and resilience. Beyond societal conditioning, these wounds can stem from various sources, including childhood experiences, relationship struggles, and unprocessed traumas. Recognizing and acknowledging these wounds is crucial, as they profoundly impact men's well-being and ability to cultivate healthy relationships and find fulfillment.

Unaddressed emotional wounds and traumas can manifest in various ways, affecting a man's life. These wounds often contribute to low self-esteem, disconnection, difficulty forming intimate relationships, and challenges managing emotions effectively. Moreover, the consequences of unhealed wounding can extend beyond individual well-being and impact families, communities, and society.

Many of us grew to be constricted men who lacked access to our emotions, the ability to express empathy and compassion, and the capacity to love unconditionally. We had lost touch with parts of ourselves we denied because they didn't match our internalized image of who we should be.

We often looked for external validation from our parents, peers, friends, and those we were attracted to romantically and/or sexually. Yet many of us internalized messages that told us we needed to go it alone.

Here's the paradox: we can't see ourselves or the truth of who we are without being in a community where we get genuine and honest feedback about how we show up. At the same time, many of us received messages that looking within is not something men do. Many of us walk around unconscious to our truth (the essence of our highest selves and our deep wounding). It's usually not until our lives go off the rails (divorce, failed relationships, bankruptcy, suicidal ideation, job loss, deafening loneliness, hitting rock bottom from addiction, etc.) that we are brought to a breaking point and realize we must start looking within and let the healing begin. From this point, we start to heal the wounds that drove our lives and took us further from our truth.

Addressing and healing emotional wounds is a transformative journey that requires courage, vulnerability, and self-compassion. At the same time, healing our wounds doesn't have to emasculate men. On the contrary, healing our wounds strengthens men to become more confident in their skin, deepen their relationships and friendships, excel on the job, and contribute more significantly to the world. It will, however, ask men to be curious and open to seeing themselves and the world in new ways.

This book offers a roadmap for men's healing based on highlights from my journey and the conversations I've had with men at the forefront of the men's healing movement. These men include therapists, men's coaches, men's health policy researchers, spiritual advisors, and those who have shared openly about their healing journeys.

The Origins of *Warrior Compassion* and the Soul-Healing Roadmap

Before launching my business, I served as the head of personal transformation and well-being for EILEEN FISHER, a socially conscious women's fashion company. In that role, I noticed how the culture transformed men. I'll share more of this journey throughout the book, but as I write about men's healing, I'll share insights and experiences from my own healing journey that helped shape the steps along the soul-healing roadmap.

In 2015, while on vacation in Barcelona, I distinctly remember sitting in a park in front of the University of Barcelona and hearing this message that kept pounding in my head:

> "As men, we've not been socialized to socialize in healthy ways."

This trip to Barcelona was my first vacation working at the fashion company after leaving Wall Street. In that park, I was experiencing what I'd describe as the deafening sound of loneliness even though people surrounded me. I was scared and felt hopeless, which was even more pronounced because I was on vacation in one of the most beautiful cities in the world. This was one of a few wake-up calls that brought me onto my healing journey. It was also one of the first times I began to connect the dots between my experience and what I saw for men across the board.

Understanding Men's Wounding

Many men I've spoken with have shared feelings of disconnect and loneliness. They would further describe the impact for them with some variation of a lack of friendships, unfulfilling sexual or romantic relationships, or a limited sense of community or belonging. I remember sitting in a men's circle, and I used the phrase "deafening sound of loneliness" to describe one of my experiences. A man across the room shouted he'd been experiencing this for years but didn't have the words.

The US surgeon general, Vivek Murthy, just released his study on the epidemic of loneliness in America (Murthy 2023). The study illustrates that loneliness is far more than just a bad feeling; it harms individual and societal health. It is associated with a greater risk of cardiovascular disease, dementia, stroke, depression, anxiety, and premature death.

The mortality impact of being socially disconnected is like that caused by smoking up to fifteen cigarettes a day. It is even more significant than that associated with obesity and physical inactivity. And the harmful consequences of a society that lacks social connection can be felt in our schools, workplaces, and civic organizations, where performance, productivity, and engagement become diminished.

In their 2023 report on the "State of American Men," Equimundo, a Washington, DC-based NGO, committed to engaging men and boys around healthy masculinity, found that 65 percent of men aged eighteen to twenty-three say, "No one knows me well." According to Equimundo, this calls for more honest, grounded, connected, and meaningful lives. This study asks for all of us to show compassion to men and build and support healthy, connected versions of manhood for the good of all (Equimundo 2023).

As men, we often live as wounded warriors, whether we want to or not. The statistics are grave, suggesting the types of pain many men can and do, experience at some point in their lives. Here are a few examples:

- According to the US Census Bureau, men in the US are less likely than women to attain a bachelor's degree, and the numbers are declining. In 2021, of adults aged twenty-five and older who had completed a bachelor's degree or more, 53.1 percent were women, and 46.9 percent were men (US Census Bureau 2022).
- In May 2021, the Survey Center on American Life revealed the number of American men who view themselves as having "no close friends" quintupled over the last thirty years, increasing from 3 percent in 1990 to 15 percent in 2021 (Cox 2021).
- According to Cigna Health Insurance, 61 percent of Americans report feeling lonely, whereas the study shows that men express more loneliness than women. The American Perspectives Survey found that men are also less likely than women to receive emotional support from their friends but more emotional support when they have female friends (Cigna Group 2023).
- According to the National Survey on Drug Use and Health (NSDUH), men battle substance abuse or dependency at rates about double those of women, 10.8 percent versus 5.8 percent, respectively (NIMH 2022).
- According to the US Center for Disease Control, the rate of suicide is highest in middle-aged white men, and in 2019, men died by suicide 3.63 times as often as women (CDC n.d.).

Over the last seven years, I've asked men what brought them to their healing journeys. Usually, a turning point in their lives propelled them to begin walking a healing journey and making significant changes. Some of the most common reasons they shared looked something like this:

- They had played the game and achieved significant financial and career success, but something was missing, and they felt unfulfilled.
- They were experiencing a deep and painful sense of loneliness, felt disconnected from others, and lacked a sense of belonging and community.
- They had hit rock bottom with alcohol, drug abuse, or sex and started working the steps in a recovery program.
- They experienced a painful breakup or failed relationship, and the pain of the heartbreak from that loss was too great and overwhelming.
- They realized they were drifting aimlessly without an anchor and didn't have a sense of meaning or purpose.
- They were living a facade and projecting an image to the world that didn't feel authentic and was no longer serving them.
- They lost themselves trying to be what others expected of them, and the disconnection was becoming too great.

From Wounding to Healing

I call these examples the plight of the wounded warrior. All humans are wounded on some level; however, men often approach healing differently from women. The big difference between the genders often centers around stigma and conditioning. The "go it alone" mindset many men embrace has often prevented them from asking for help. At the same time, asking for help is stigmatized as a sign of weakness for men.

Men also tend to have less access to healing experiences than women. Many men have told me they didn't know what was available in their healing journey beyond therapy. So, men continue to walk the path of the wounded warrior until they hit a turning point in their lives that takes them in a new direction.

Many men I've spoken with described the healing process as coming home to the truth and essence of who they are. As I think about it, we return to our full humanity and become whole again. By whole, I mean who we were the moment we came out of the womb. At that time, we had everything within us—our creativity, imagination, joy, curiosity, access to our full range of emotions, sensitivity, and ability to love unconditionally without judgment, expectations, or conditions. Then life happened.

As we grew up, some parts of ourselves became suppressed or got beaten out of us, often based on what we were taught, socialized, or conditioned. We began to internalize these messages, further defining our identity, worldview, and how we should show up in the world. The healing journey to return to our whole selves isn't linear, is rarely easy, and can be painful. It requires courage, surrender, patience, and support.

As you continue reading this book, I want to instill one crucial message: as a man, you are not broken. At the same time, you very well might be wounded. Underlying this message is an important distinction where we shift the narrative from men who are broken to men who have been injured.

You don't need to fix what's broken, but you can heal what's wounded. However, most men don't have the opportunities (either because of access, stigma, or we don't permit ourselves) to look at and heal our wounds. This book offers a roadmap to healing the suffering holding us back from living a meaningful life that reflects our truth.

At the end of each chapter, I'll ask you a series of reflective questions. Think of each chapter as another step in the roadmap for healing and the questions at the end of each chapter as thought-provoking reflections to help you deepen your understanding of yourself as you walk your path.

As you think about your journey, consider the following questions:

- When you look in the mirror, what do you see that the rest of the world doesn't?
- Having read this chapter, in what ways do you feel you might be suffering in silence?
- What wounds are holding you back from being the best version of yourself?
- If those wounds were healed, what do you hope would change in your life?

The plight of the wounded warrior represents the challenges and struggles many men face today. From societal expectations of strength and invulnerability to the suppression of emotions, men often suffer in silence, carrying deep emotional wounds that hinder their well-being and prevent them from seeking the support they need. Healing these wounds requires courage, vulnerability, and self-compassion. By embarking on the healing journey and addressing the underlying traumas and emotional burdens, men can strengthen their authenticity and relationships, find a deeper sense of purpose, and contribute meaningfully to the world.

This book's roadmap for soul healing combines personal experiences, insights from pioneers in the men's healing movement, and thought-provoking questions to guide men on their transformative journey. It is crucial to remember men are not broken but wounded. Shifting the narrative from brokenness to woundedness allows men to embrace their capacity for healing and growth. By acknowledging and healing their wounds, men can reclaim their whole selves and live a life that reflects their authentic truth.

As you continue reading this book and exploring your own journey, remember to look within, ask yourself reflective questions, and envision the changes you hope to see in your life. By doing so, you are taking a powerful step toward healing your wounds and opening yourself up for an adventure you can't even imagine.

CHAPTER 2

WARRIOR COMPASSION
AS A HEALING POWER

───

Two days after saying my vows in seminary to become an interfaith minister, I received a video from a friend. In the video was the chief of police of the Asheville Police Department asking for community members to volunteer to participate in the police reform efforts in Asheville. Three weeks before receiving the video, I made the decision to move from Spanish Harlem, New York City, to West Asheville, North Carolina.

In seminary, they told us when you hear the call, you say yes, no matter what. The following day, I emailed the chief of police directly. I opened my note by saying I would be moving from New York City to Asheville in three weeks, and my best friend in London would visit me in New York but was afraid to visit me in Asheville because he was afraid of being murdered by the police.

I shared that I know most police officers are there to truly serve and protect and that North Carolina has the least police shootings of any state in the South. However, my British friend kept hearing about police killing black men and women in America. I finished by saying I had to be part of these efforts because I couldn't assure my friend of his safety.

That letter and my credentials led to a one-on-one conversation with the police chief. In our in-person meeting, he had two asks:

1. Could I help him deepen the level of compassion among his officers?
2. Could I create conversations between police officers and community members to humanize each other for a new relationship going forward?

I said yes to both requests. This became the foundation for my work with police and men in hypermasculine cultures and systems. It also spurred the idea for the title *Warrior Compassion*, originally named *The Compassionate Masculinity Project*, when I started on this path. I've found on this journey that by saying yes, doors open that you can't even imagine. By saying yes to the police chief, a group of us from across the country found each other and formed what we call Project Compassion, a national initiative to bring a deeper level of compassion into police departments.

The Power of Compassion

When we combine the concepts of warrior and compassion, an energetic shift happens. According to the *Cambridge Dictionary*, "Compassion is most easily defined as the feeling or emotion when a person is moved by the suffering or distress of another, and by the desire to relieve its suffering" (Oxford

English Dictionary 2023). Taking a step further, to be compassionate to others, we must begin by learning to become compassionate with ourselves.

According to Ed Adams and Ed Frauenheim, authors and masculinity experts, "Compassion means, literally, to feel with others. To experience the distress of another and act to alleviate or end that distress. Through compassion, the liberating man helps himself and others find purpose, peace, and genuine satisfaction. Compassion is about men letting their hearts be touched—even broken—by suffering and then working to relieve that suffering or prevent it in the first place" (Adams and Frauenheim 2020).

The Strength of the Warrior Spirit

The warrior archetype represents strength, courage, and the relentless pursuit of justice and honor. It embodies discipline, resilience, and unwavering determination to protect and defend what is most valued. The warrior archetype is not limited to physical combat but extends to the inner battle against adversity and the commitment to personal growth and the greater good.

For this book, I will ask you to hold the image of the warrior as that courageous spirit within us that is compelled to defend and protect something sacred. In this definition, I'm asking you to suspend your idea that the warrior is solely an identity and see it as more of an energy within each of us. The warrior spirit will fight for what's right and what's just and shield those who need protection. This speaks to the fierce intensity of the warrior energy.

Recently, I was asked why I'm calling wounded men wounded warriors. The short answer is that the archetype of the wounded warrior represents men who have experienced emotional, psychological, or physical wounds due to their life experiences, particularly in the context of conflict, trauma, or adversity. This archetype provides a lens through which we can explore the challenges, struggles, and healing journeys of men who have been wounded in various ways.

Focusing on the archetype of wounded warriors, we acknowledge men's resilience and strength despite their wounds. We recognize their inner warrior spirit and their capacity for transformation and healing. This perspective allows us to approach their healing journey with compassion, understanding, and a desire to support their personal growth and well-being.

I had a conversation with Joe Laur, one of the elders of the men's movement. Joe is a friend and has been a mentor to me over the years. He was an early executive director of the ManKind Project in the late 1980s. When discussing the definition of the warrior, he shared, "To me, it means walking the edge of the knife or the edge of the sword. It means setting boundaries. And if necessary, defending those boundaries in an appropriate way. It means serving something greater than myself so I have a guiding light, a true north that I can follow. And the world also needs a well-developed lover with a compassionate side. Warriors can't be headless or heartless. But to me, that's the essence of it. As I think of the word warrior, I think of the knife edge cutting through the bullshit. Cutting through the confusion. Bringing clarity."

Defining Warrior Compassion

When we bring the warrior spirit to compassion, it becomes a courageous and loving energy that brings healing to the suffering. I define warrior compassion as:

> The fierce healing power within that liberates you to courageously walk from a place of deeper consciousness, compassion, and connection in the world while expanding creativity, authenticity, intimacy, and a sense of community in the ways you live and carry out your mission.

Take a moment to digest this definition. It might feel overwhelming or a lot to take in and process. Another way to think about warrior compassion is that it's a force deep within you (it's always been there) waiting to come to the surface when you are ready. When you walk a healing path, you'll begin to access this force, which can transform your life and how you see and experience the world.

Warrior compassion can be a catalyst that helps men evolve from the wounded warrior to the healing warrior. A healing warrior is someone who is engaged in their healing journey. It's important to note that once you open the door to this path, it never stops, and seeds are planted along the way germinating in their own time with the right conditions, cultivation, and timing. This type of healing begins to tackle the wounds that keep us disconnected, isolated, and lonely.

Warrior compassion is the healing power we need to be courageous enough to walk the healing journey and look at the parts of ourselves we don't want to see—those places where we are afraid to look at ourselves honestly and, more importantly, the areas where we experience intense and extreme shame. This path is about getting curious to look beneath the layers of fear and shame to the profound wounding or trauma constricting men.

(Image: Harvey 2023)

My Connection to Warrior Compassion

Warrior compassion was introduced to me at an early age. Every night before bed, my Cherokee grandfather would tell me the stories of Little Red Chief. My grandfather was a first-generation truck driver and a decorated veteran who served directly under General Patton in World War II. He truly blended the gruffness of men of his time and a compassionate heart that stemmed from his Cherokee roots and his deep faith in God.

I remember one of his stories, where Little Red Chief, a young Cherokee boy, was being trained and guided by the warriors and elders of his tribe to become a fierce warrior. One night around the fire, he was told that to defend and protect his community, he needed to embrace the power of compassion. He had a God-given responsibility to demonstrate love and understanding to every person he encountered.

Even to his greatest adversary whom he would go to war with, he must show love and compassion and strive to see the humanity in the man in front of him. At the same time, he can only demonstrate love and understanding to his adversary by first showing the same love for himself.

As I reflect, my grandfather told me the stories of a boy being given challenges as part of his training to strengthen as a compassionate and loving man. Becoming a man who is a fierce defender and protector of others by having an open heart, witnessing, and taking action to address and eliminate one's suffering while embracing a caring approach to others. At four years old, my Cherokee grandfather told me these stories to help me tap into my compassionate heart for everyone I met, those I hadn't known, and all living beings and creatures on this planet.

The Healing Power of Warrior Compassion

Yet compassion is often seen as a sign of weakness because, as men, many of us have internalized the message that we have to be strong, we can't show emotions or vulnerability, and we must strive to be the best. I want to return to the idea that we can't show emotions. When we've been told and internalized that we can't show or express emotions, the consequence is that we often can't feel emotions. It becomes difficult to empathize with others and show compassion when we cannot feel our full range of emotions. The messages we've internalized and the wounds we've experienced keep us from feeling.

I remember hearing this message at a Human Interaction Lab I attended several years ago that still sits with me:

"As men, we will intellectualize and rationalize our way out of feeling."

When we intellectualize or rationalize our way out of feeling, we often cannot access our full range of emotions and feelings, let alone express them—making it difficult, if not impossible, to be empathetic and compassionate. This is yet another reason it's crucial to engage in our healing journeys. To access our full range of emotions, we must deconstruct the messages and heal the wounds that have prevented us from feeling those emotions.

When we ignore our emotions, we still have them. We must ask ourselves, will we control our emotions, or will our emotions control us? The healing work enables us to evolve from our knee-jerk reactions to engage with more thoughtful responses. Otherwise, we might:

- Sit with our judgments of others or ourselves.
- Get defensive when we are triggered by something that activates our emotions.
- Stand our ground in an unmovable way because we are challenged.
- Need to be right and stand in our righteousness.
- Shrink or check out when the feelings overwhelm us.
- Lash out or pick a fight.
- Act out with sex, drugs, alcohol, work, food, spending, gambling, etc.

Ultimately, *Warrior Compassion* intends to teach men to love fully and unconditionally. It begins with self-love and compassion, which includes reclaiming those parts of themselves riddled with shame, disgust, or rage. Walking this path, they become less critical of themselves and others and move into a place of greater acceptance. These are the foundational building blocks to elevate empathy and compassion. From here, men can begin to experience a different level of empathy for the suffering that others are experiencing—in relationships, friendships, with parents, in communities, organizations, and society.

As we begin our healing journeys, our stuff that isn't pretty can make us feel wildly uncomfortable when it touches the places where we hold our greatest shame. The unfortunate part of the healing journey is that we must experience the discomfort to move to the edges of healing and growth, to evolve into the men we were meant to become.

So, why would anyone go on this journey if it would be painful and uncomfortable? Think of a healing journey as a soul adventure where you don't quite know the destination, but the journey is worth the price of admission. Most men I've spoken with could never have imagined where they would end up after beginning their adventure.

Ken Mossman, a well-respected men's coach, offers a unique men's personal growth approach called "I AM," which stands for "integrated adult male." Ken shared his thoughts about a man's readiness for walking the healing path and said, "You are ready when you're ready, and not a moment before. It requires a nonattachment that allows the journey to take shape in its time."

As I think about my journey, each time I began to listen to that voice within, I would have a "knowing" about the next step. When I say knowing, I'm suggesting that intuitive or inner knowing that comes from accessing more profound wisdom that transcends logic. I knew the next step aligned with who I was and what I valued most, yet the intense emotions and the discomfort passes, and things begin to normalize. At the same time, I'd look up and realize my world looked different, and I viewed the world through a new lens.

Think of the healing journey as an adventure that opens the door to liberation and freedom to be the person you are meant to be. As you evolve into your liberated self, the expectations of who you should be and the standards you've held yourself to are released. The constraints you placed on yourself that have constricted your life are lifted.

Your self-worth elevates in ways that the opinions of others have less of an impact on you, and you can give yourself the validation you've been seeking from others. You stop needing to prove yourself and begin to accept yourself for who you are now and not for the idea of who you should be. In a sense, you get to rewrite your own script of who you are and how you want to live your life. This journey can liberate men to:

- Discover and learn to love the truth of who they are.
- Show up in the world differently with greater ease and joy.
- Reclaim parts of themselves they have suppressed or rejected.
- Own the full range of emotions and not be taken hostage by feelings.
- Develop healthier relationships and a greater sense of intimacy.
- Deepen nurturing guidance and love as fathers and partners.
- Discover a deeper sense of purpose and meaning in life.

As you can see, the potential long-term benefits far outweigh the discomfort. That said, I've talked to many men who have expressed a fear of opening "Pandora's box." They fear the emotions will be overwhelming or what they discover will be so wrong or bad they won't recover. Once they unleash their feelings, they will lose control. At the same time, they often experience an inherent fear of being emasculated and feeling like less of a man by walking this path. From experience, it's quite the opposite, where this journey can make a man feel stronger, more confident, and in control of his destiny. However, the healing path can be disconcerting as it challenges your notions of who you are and how you see the world—a deidentification, if you will.

What I can't express enough is that a critical element of any transformation journey is to have the courage to surrender control. This is very difficult for most of us to do, especially for men, where they feel a need to remain in control. You can think of the journey as an adventure that requires you to have the courage to walk into the unknown without an understanding or control of where the path will take you. If you dare to step into the unknown, lean into the discomfort, and let go of the messages and beliefs that have limited and constricted you, you might be ready to walk your healing journey.

As you think about your journey, I ask you to consider the following:

- What does warrior compassion mean to you?
- In what ways do you experience and embrace your warrior spirit?
- In what ways do you express compassion for yourself and others?
- What do you hope is possible when you embrace warrior compassion as a healing path?

Walking into the unknown is a hallmark of transformation as we evolve from one way of being into another. Think of this journey as the metamorphosis. The healing journey can help us grow into a version of ourselves that is beautiful, powerful, and full of possibility. The healing journey also helps elevate our energetic vibration by shifting us into a deeper level of consciousness, an expanded ability to love, and wisdom that taps into our hearts and souls.

As a professor, I would always tell my students I'm not teaching them rocket science but rather common-sense practices that aren't commonly practiced. This book is designed to help you see and access what's been inside you all along. You have the capacity to feel deeply, love unconditionally, accept yourself fully, and embrace others with fierce compassion. It's already inside you; you just need to tap into it and let it out into the world.

PART II

UNPACKING MY HEALING JOURNEY

———

Men's Compassionate Heart Prayer

—SEAN HARVEY, INTERFAITH AND
INTERSPIRITUAL MINISTER

Divine Spirit, we ask that you bless each man walking his
    sacred path.
Help him find the gifts of his hardships and struggles from
    his past.
Let your loving light shine down upon his heart and soul.
Open his heart to its greatest depths of compassion.

Free his mind to receive your wisdom and truth.
Let his free mind and open heart sit together in your light.
Remove any wounds preventing his heart from feeling.
Walk beside each man in his struggle and offer him hope.

Replace any fear or shame with love and splendor.
Help him see the world with childlike wonder.
Illuminate each of his steps with your light and love.
Allow his compassionate heart to shine freely in the world.

CHAPTER 3

MY HEALING JOURNEY AT EILEEN FISHER

———

My healing journey started on my fortieth birthday when I resigned as the vice president of a talent consulting division for a boutique consulting firm serving Wall Street and big media clients in New York City. I was burned out and felt utterly unfulfilled at that point in my life. I remember telling the firm's CEO I had lost my heart and soul in the job, and it was time for me to move on.

Two weeks later, a friend told me about an internal organizational development consulting role opening at EILEEN FISHER (EF)—the socially-conscious women's fashion company I mentioned earlier—and I decided to apply. This led to an eight-month interview process, in which I met with twenty-seven people in six group interviews, completed a case study, and facilitated three internal consulting engagements. While this was a lengthy interview process, it gave me a sense of the company, and I realized I was entering an entirely different type of organization.

As I listened to my intuition, the message was unmistakable I had to work for this company. I had no question or doubt in my mind. I honestly didn't know why, and I didn't know where the path would take me. I just knew deep down that I had to make the transition. I was stepping into the unknown and walking into the mystery with only the guidance of my inner knowing, or as I like to call it now, my sacred compass.

On my first day on the job at EF, my two bosses sat me down and said:

> "Sean, you have proven yourself over the eight-month interview process, and now we want you to stop proving yourself. During the interview process, you showed us your heart and your polish. We hired you for your heart and want to see less of your polish. We want you to find the authentic you, and we'll support you in the messiness of finding the real you. We want to see Sean unfiltered."

This conversation was a pivotal moment in my journey that changed the course and trajectory of my life. First, who says this in a work setting? And second, this was permission to explore who I was at my authentic core. I had two highly intuitive and compassionate bosses and a team who saw me. They fully embraced me as they witnessed me and experienced my gifts and flaws.

That polish they mentioned was how I thought I was supposed to show up at work and in the world. It was my ego wanting to be seen and to shine, and at the same time, it was telling me I wasn't enough. My response was to overcompensate for my insecurities through an unrealistic level of perfectionism, where I felt I had to compete to be better than others. My identity was wrapped up in my accomplishments and my achievements, which became my calling card in most interactions.

My five years at the company introduced me to my journey to become unfiltered, discover the real me, and accept my true self. This path allows me to share my lessons learned with other men. I'll share a few wild and mind-blowing experiences while working at EF. Throughout my five years at the fashion company, one of my bosses would say two phrases repeatedly:

1. "You're here for a reason, and it's not the job. In time, you'll figure out why."
2. "When you come to the company and stay, you'll be transformed by the company."

Creative Facilitation and Interpretative Dance

It was May 2014, and I remember sitting in Eileen Fisher's living room at a two-day creative training retreat with most of my leadership, learning, and development team members. As you continue reading this book, EILEEN FISHER is used to describe the company, and Eileen Fisher is used to describe the founder. We were learning to incorporate the arts (song, dance, drawing, painting, arts and crafts, spoken word/poetry, improv, and games) into our creative facilitation techniques to enrich creativity with our teams.

Two-and-a-half hours into the experience, while drums were beating in the background, I found myself doing interpretive dance as a tree blowing in the wind to a poem co-written by my colleague. It was read aloud in spoken word poetry called *Bumble Bee Trying to Find Her Nectar.* As a former high school and college cheerleader, I was familiar with dance routines. However, interpretive dance at work was a new experience. After our performance, my boss chuckled as she approached me and said, "You know you're in a different world now, right?"

A different world was right, and it was nothing I could have imagined. As a man who left a successful consulting career serving Wall Street and big media companies to come to EF and get a one-of-a-kind in-house experience, I was in for the ride of my life (professionally and personally).

I began working as the internal change agent for creative and later the company's head of purpose, personal transformation, and well-being during my tenure. At the time, EF was a B Corp women's clothing company with roughly $425 million in annual revenue and twelve-hundred employees across the US, UK, and Canada. The company was comprised of 83 percent women and subscribed fully and unapologetically to feminine leadership principles and practices.

We Do Things Differently Around Here

For my first three and a half years at EF, I engaged with highly creative teams (design, merchandising, brand communications, social consciousness, and web/e-commerce) around change, leadership development, and team forming and alignment. My work was driven by a culture that supports creative energy flow. We did this by remaining organic, less focused on outcomes, and more on inclusive and collaborative discussions that brought in different voices for greater democratic decision-making. We often played in the tension of the dualities of intuition versus data, creative versus business, organic versus structure, and complexity versus simplicity.

We also had several rituals in which we engaged that helped to create the container for our culture. All meetings started with silence and meditation to create space for everyone to come into the room and become fully present for each other. Every conference room throughout the company had singing bowls. Following the silence, teams would engage in an individual personal and professional check-in to get a read of the emotional energy coming into the space that may impact the attention and agenda of the meeting.

We also used the "circle way," where we would meet in circles with no tables between us, to break down the energy of hierarchy and allow all voices to be heard, often with a circle check-in and round-robin conversations. We used a mantra that Eileen often shared in many meetings, which was "perfect enough" so we could move away from perfectionism to prototyping, trying new ideas, and allowing for greater innovation.

In my role, you could have called me the retreat guy. During my second year on the job, I counted that I had designed and facilitated fifty-six full days of retreats and offsites. I had so many retreats at EF that I sometimes designed a full-day experience in a thirty-seven-minute train ride from Harlem to Irvington, New York. Unknowingly, I was mastering my craft of facilitation in the process while creating powerful experiences that brought people together in new ways and allowed collective wisdom to emerge.

I still remember the day I was walking through downtown Irvington with a stuffed elephant under my arm for the "elephant in the room" conversations. This was another moment when I couldn't believe this was my job, but I loved every minute of it.

Exposure to Unconventional Experiences

I've been fortunate to have had some life-changing experiences throughout my time at EF, which included (Harvey 2019):

- Attending a five-day Human Interaction Lab (HI Lab) in Virginia during my first year to examine and enhance my emotional intelligence and challenge and transform limiting beliefs.
- Spending five weekends over five months at an artist commune in Canada with artists and youth empowerment facilitators to get a more profound experience of integrating an arts-based approach into facilitation design and delivery as a pathway to deeper transformation work with our employees.
- Co-creating a personal transformation and growth experience that introduces our employees to their life purpose and deeper self-awareness using the enneagram assessment, somatic/embodiment work, shadow work, limiting beliefs work, and spirit/mindfulness practices.
- Serving as a volunteer facilitator for the boys' program (fifteen- to seventeen-year-olds) of the Eileen Fisher Leadership Institute, delivering a workshop challenging traditional masculinity models called "Lessons from our Fathers, Letters to our Dads."
- Being guided by our in-house Akashic records reader, medical intuitive, and astrologer (available to all employees).

EF offered employees access to many teachers and healers through our EF LIFEWORK programs, including Shadow and Purpose workshops.

- Holding space as a trusted ally to design and facilitate our "We the Change: Women Together" planning retreat bringing together the voices of our women's empowerment facilitators as they partnered to carry out Eileen's vision of creating a global women's empowerment movement.

Healing the Masculine through the Feminine

Throughout my EF experience, I learned to deepen my listening, create space more deliberately for different voices, and appreciate the significance of language and the power of words. More importantly, I learned the power of simplicity, spaciousness, and silence. Eventually, I learned to relax my ego and let go of the need to prove my worth and value. I began to quiet my voice and listen differently. I could see and accept other points of view without needing to be right or coming off as righteous.

I've developed the patience to sit with and hold space for deep contemplation of issues and challenges without feeling the need to rush to solve the problem or find the answer. By letting go of the restrictions I've placed on myself as a man and based on my conditioning, I've allowed my emotional and creative expression to come through more fully while tapping into my intuitive abilities.

I've worked diligently with my leaders and wellness director to examine work/life balance. As a former consultant, I didn't see the need for the life part of work/life balance. This included looking at self-care in new ways around diet, exercise, and healthier lifestyles. Where I noticed the most remarkable change in my life was in my relationships. As a former introverted workaholic, I've learned to value relationships and friendships in new and profound ways. Our collaborative environment encouraged that type of transformation of relationships and way of being with others.

I attribute these shifts to my journey through the feminine that ultimately strengthened me in my masculine. At EF, we distinguished between the masculine and feminine energies in the following ways (Harvey 2020):

The Healthy Feminine	The Healthy Masculine
Authenticity	Direct communication
Collaboration	Sense of purpose and vision
Heart-centered leadership	Head-centered leadership
Trust in intuition	Clear strategies and goals
Emotional and creative expression	Results and action orientation
Ensure all voices are heard	Logical and analytical frameworks
Compassionate conflict	Constructive assertiveness

As an organization, we acknowledged we needed both energies in the corporate culture, ultimately creating a conscious, compassionate, and connected environment. We had a saying that we spoke the truth with kindness as our primary way of relating with each other. When we identified ideal leaders, we asked that they balance healthy masculine and healthy feminine attributes. In my healing journey, I began to embody the balance and integration of the two energies.

As I consider the healing journeys for men, I argue every man can hold the qualities of each energy if he is willing to embark on his healing journey to reclaim and access the parts of himself he denied, rejected, or ostracized. Throughout the book, I'll continue to reiterate that integrating the feminine does not make you weak but strengthens your masculine. By integrating my feminine, I would say my expression and energy became even more masculine. I let go of any insecurities about not being man enough, and I was able to be more comfortable in my own skin and adapt to situations easily.

Working with the Akashic Records

While at EF, I worked with an Akashic records reader, who was available to all employees as part of well-being offerings. In addition to the Akashic reader, we had access to a medical intuitive, astrologer, massage therapists, chiropractors, acupuncturists, and Ayurvedic lunches.

An Akashic records reader is an intuitive guide who has developed the ability to access and interpret sacred soul records, a metaphysical realm believed to contain all souls' collective knowledge and experiences. Think of it as a soul-DNA record that travels with you across lifetimes.

Through deep meditation and trance, the reader connects with this energetic database to retrieve information about past lives, present circumstances, and future potentials. They serve as intermediaries between the seeker and the Akashic records, providing insights, guidance, and healing based on the information that accedes. These records offer a pathway for individuals to gain clarity, find answers to their most profound questions, and facilitate personal growth and spiritual transformation.

About once a quarter, I'd typically see June Brought, the Akashic records reader at EF. She would provide powerful insights during each session. However, in one session, I remember vividly her telling me:

> "Sean, it's great that you have a vision and a plan; now I want you to walk out of your masculine and into your feminine and walk from a place of curiosity and wonderment and let go of the need to control the outcome."

This straightforward message helped me better understand the distinctions between masculine and feminine energies from within in a practical way that didn't feel scary or emasculating. Working with June helped to center and ground me. She was the first of many spiritual guides I would encounter and work with along this journey.

My Time at the Artist Commune

Three years into my tenure at the fashion company, I was sent to an artist community (or, as I like to say, the artist commune) in Kingston, Ontario, to learn how to incorporate the arts into creative facilitation. The program took place over five long weekends over five months.

Throughout my time in Kingston, I would engage with various facilitation practices that helped me tap into my artistic abilities as a facilitator through creative methods. This included storytelling, play, dance, drawing, painting, games, movement, breathwork, poetry, etc. These practices became a foundational dimension of my work with men by helping them let their guard down and tap into their deeper intuition.

During the first weekend in a Sunday morning visualization exercise, I saw my life flash before my eyes, and I realized I had been uniquely designed to work with men on their healing. I left Wall Street consulting because I didn't want to work with men. So, hearing this call to work with men, I knew this was beyond my pay grade and must be some sort of spiritual calling.

The message I received during my vacation in Barcelona was the first time I heard the call to work with men, and the first weekend in Kingston was the second time I heard the call. The funny thing about a spiritual calling is you can't not pursue it. What I've learned over the last seven years of this journey is when I ignore the call, my life gets exponentially more difficult until I get back onto the path and continue to engage in my healing work to create an inner alignment.

Nurturing the Soul of the Company at EILEEN FISHER

In addition, I co-authored an article with two researchers called "Nurturing the Soul of the Company at EILEEN FISHER" for the *Journal of Management, Spirituality, and Religion*. In our interviews, we asked employees how they defined the company's soul. It was clear to many employees who said the founder, Eileen Fisher, embodied the company's soul. They would describe how she made decisions by trusting the deep intuitive knowing more than the evidence-based empirical data (Betters-Reed, Harvey, and Neal 2020).

A company's soul stems from the leader and the deeply held beliefs of that leader. An alignment of deeply held values and beliefs created a robust culture of generosity, simplicity, quality of life, compassion, curiosity, consciousness, creativity, and humanity-based connection.

Co-authoring the article and being surrounded by spiritual teachers and guides at the company were key contributors as I decided to apply to an interfaith seminary. Following my intuition again, I knew that if I was going to work with men, it had to be at a soul-healing level.

For my path, psychological counseling or coaching wasn't the only answer for men; my calling was asking me to engage men around their spiritual and soul-healing growth. I earned my master's degree in counseling and have the psychological training needed. But for this path, a soul-healing roadmap requires a psychospiritual approach.

Leading Personal Transformation at EF

In my third year at EF, I began transitioning into a new role, co-creating and delivering a leadership program focused on purpose and personal transformation. This cutting-edge program introduced the enneagram, strengths finder, ego relaxation, somatic (embodied movement) practices, mindfulness/contemplative practices, healing the shadow, transforming limiting beliefs, and discovering purpose. All employees were invited to participate in this program, and a similar program was offered to all leaders.

I also created an additional program to support leaders in guiding and supporting their employees through the purpose journey. In some cases, employees discovered their life purpose existed outside of EF, and we honored their journey and gracefully helped them exit the company to pursue their purpose.

As we began to unearth deeper wounds through this work, we focused on three areas for employees to explore: unmet needs, limiting beliefs, and shadow. Underlying these wounds were the unhealed trauma that employees and leaders brought into the workplace. While this was cutting edge, Eileen believed in this work as she shared with the employees what worked for her on her journey. In a sense, I'm following Eileen's model and sharing the reflections and wisdom of my journey with other men to see another possible path to explore and examine their healing.

"Lessons from Our Fathers, Letters to Our Dads"

I had the opportunity to lead a session on healthy masculinity for teenage boys from across the country as part of the Eileen Fisher Leadership Institute experience for high school students. The session was "Lessons from Our Fathers, Letters to Our Dads." This session was the culmination of experiences at EF and the work I was jumping into around redefining manhood, healthy masculinity, compassionate healing through the integrated feminine, and men's personal transformation journeys.

On the morning I was to lead the first session, I received a phone call that my father had passed away a few hours earlier. Receiving the news on the day I led this session felt somewhat poetic as we had healed our relationship over the last year after fourteen years of not speaking. It was the weekend prior when I had driven to Detroit to see my father before he entered hospice care.

Leading this session, I knew my father was with me on this journey, and our reconnection story inspired this conversation. Hearing the teenage boys talk about their relationships with their fathers further clarified how complex the father/son relationship can be. Each young man shared what he had been taught about what it means to be a man by his father or the father figure in his life. There was no judgment around the lessons learned from the fathers. Then he would describe on the back of the letter the man he aspired to become as an adult. It was a powerful exercise, and it further demonstrated the level of influence fathers have on their sons in their presence and their absence. It also highlighted how young men see the world differently from their fathers.

Understanding the Man's Experience at EF

As a man working in a fashion company that was 83 percent women and valued compassion, creativity, and deep connection, I started noticing how the culture transformed me and later witnessed how it transformed other men. I would ask men in corporate and at the creative center if they thought they were changing. The men would typically answer, "Well, my wife (or girlfriend) said that…

- I listened differently."
- I was more patient."
- I had more tolerance for nuanced conversations."
- I stopped needing to be right all the time and started to be more curious."

- I was more comfortable in the gray and moved beyond black-and-white thinking."
- I was more emotionally expressive."
- I checked my ego at the door and was more open-minded."

Each man would also talk about how he noticed he was more creative and could solve problems differently. Each man also spoke about creating more space for those who didn't look like him. What seemed most significant was that each man shared how he was more comfortable in his own skin and navigating the world more effortlessly. Life didn't feel like such a chore, and he could relax, have fun, and enjoy life more.

I had a similar experience. I also felt more comfortable in my own skin. Every day I was letting go of years of old conditioning and tapes that had stemmed from messages about how I needed to show up as a man and my limiting beliefs around the ways I didn't measure up to the ideal in my head of what it means to be a man.

I knew we were onto something here, and a model for men's healing through the feminine needed to be shared with other men and organizations worldwide.

Launching the Compassionate Masculinity Project

In December 2018, I left EF to start my company, Sympónia Studios. Sympónia is the Greek word for compassion. My work on men's healing started as The Compassionate Masculinity Project.

I launched my company and the project with three underlying questions driving the exploration:

1. What becomes possible if more men have access to the journey that the other two hundred men at EF and I experienced?
2. How might we innovate and solve problems differently if we were able to create more gender balance in the workplace where the voices of women and the feminine were elevated on par with men's voices and the masculine?
3. How might we reimagine leadership models, team design, systems and structures, and workplace culture if we take a more integrated approach that balances the healthy masculine and feminine in the workplace?

With these three questions, I would embark on a soul adventure of a lifetime that would challenge me to the depths of my being. I had more dark nights of the soul during this next chapter of my life than I can count. I built the resilience for the work ahead because of those challenging times. I had begun walking the path of my soul's calling. I was on a soul adventure.

As you think about your journey, I ask you to consider the following:

- What aspects of my journey resonate for you as you think about your journey?
- When you reflect on how EF transformed men, what shifts attract you?
- What experiences have you had that introduced you to a more authentic you?
- What experiences have challenged you to think differently about yourself and the world?

My time at EF was a transformative period in my life. I embarked on a healing journey that reshaped my understanding of masculinity and allowed me to embrace my authentic self. Through the guidance and support of compassionate leaders and a culture that valued creativity, collaboration, and emotional expression, I strengthened my masculine in ways that were healed through the feminine. This journey taught me the importance of letting go of the need for perfectionism, embracing vulnerability, and cultivating deep connections with others.

I witnessed how this approach transformed myself and other men in the organization, leading to greater authenticity, creativity, and a sense of purpose. My transformation during this time is a testament to the profound impact that embracing the feminine, without fear or shame, and integrating both masculine and feminine energies can have on personal growth, relationships, and the world.

In reflecting on your journey, I encourage you to consider the resonance you feel with the experiences shared in this chapter and the shifts you find attractive and resonant. Explore the messages you receive from loved ones and the insights they offer about your own growth and potential. Embrace the moments that have introduced you to the authentic version of yourself and challenged your perspective on the world. As you navigate these questions, remember to approach them with self-love and compassion, allowing yourself the space to explore and embrace your unique healing path.

CHAPTER 4

EMBARKING ON MY SOUL ADVENTURE

—

This journey has been crazy, with so many unexpected twists and turns. I've wanted to say screw it and get a "real job" many times, but something inside just kept saying keep going; this is important as this is your soul's calling. The funny thing about a soul's calling is you don't really have a choice. Life will become progressively harder until you surrender to the call. This has been my soul adventure, and I'm on the ride of a lifetime.

What Is a Soul Adventure?

A soul adventure is a transformative journey of self-discovery, growth, and expansion that takes individuals on a deep exploration of their inner world and connection to the greater universe. It is a quest to discover the essence of one's being, purpose, and truth. In a soul adventure, individuals embark on self-exploration and embrace the unknown, stepping outside their comfort zones to tap into their authentic selves and connect with the vast possibilities within and around them.

Parker Palmer, a world-renowned author on spirituality, describes the soul as a "[w]ild animal... tough, resilient, resourceful, savvy, and self-sufficient: it knows how to survive in hard places. Yet despite its toughness, the soul is also shy" (Palmer 2004).

In this sense, a soul adventure is a path to allow the shy soul to come out to play. It may be seen as a quest for higher consciousness, spiritual enlightenment, or a deeper understanding of the interconnectedness of all things. It may involve confronting inner demons or shadow aspects of the self. A soul adventure may include meditation, mindfulness, journaling, self-reflection, and immersive experiences in nature. It may also involve embarking on physical journeys to sacred sites, participating in rituals or ceremonies, and seeking guidance from spiritual teachers or guides.

Ultimately, the purpose of a soul adventure in this context is to awaken and activate the spiritual potential within oneself, leading to a greater sense of purpose, connection, and harmony with the universe. By embarking on a soul adventure, individuals can experience profound shifts in their perspectives, beliefs, and sense of self, leading to a deeper understanding of their purpose, an expansion of consciousness, and a greater sense of interconnectedness with all of existence.

Heading to Seminary: Building a Foundation for Men's Soul Healing

At EF, I discovered my life purpose: being a healing man and helping other men heal. Living out my purpose has led to my beginning seminary, where I gained the spiritual grounding to support men's personal transformation and spiritual awakening journeys. This work challenges the traditional models and definitions of masculine identity and finds pathways to help men access and elevate the feminine, so they begin to walk in a more balanced way—holding a healthy balance of masculine and feminine energy in how they show up and be in the world.

I was never that religious as I wasn't raised in the church and my parents weren't spiritual. However, I felt a pull to find a church home around thirty-six years old. I ultimately joined Marble Collegiate Church in NYC, the longest continuously running Protestant church in North America, founded in 1628. After becoming a member, I quickly found myself moving into a lay leadership role as a group of us formed a counseling ministry in the church. I had a foundational spiritual understanding and a calling that unfolded at EF.

When I started hearing the call, I intuitively knew the work with men had to be done at a soul level. So, I was guided to enter the seminary, where I became an interfaith minister focusing on supporting men's spiritual growth journeys. Soul healing is a process of personal transformation that focuses on a person's spiritual and emotional aspects. It involves connecting with one's inner wisdom, exploring past experiences and traumas, and releasing negative emotions and limiting beliefs. Soul healing aims to promote inner peace, balance, and wholeness and to help a person live a more fulfilling and joyful life.

I experienced and worked through my soul healing on a deep level during seminary. I affectionally call seminary a journey in which you have your own unique and customized ego dissolution experience to bring you into greater consciousness and awakening of your own truth. Not every-one needs to go to seminary for their healing journey, but I'll be sharing insights from my journey throughout the book to add context and texture to these concepts surrounding soul healing.

Shamanic Journeys: Getting a Vision for Men's Healing

On my first weekend in seminary, I decided to try some-thing radical that would push me out of my comfort zone by checking out a shamanic journey. According to Sandra Ingerman, shamanic journeying is the inner art of traveling to the "invisible worlds" beyond ordinary reality to retrieve information for change in any area of our lives—from spiri-tuality and health to work and relationships (Ingerman 2012).

When I arrived in the room, the moment my foot touched the floor, I experienced a level of familiarity that felt like I'd come home, and I knew this would be an instrumental part of my journey. The room had about sixty to eighty people sitting in a circle around an altar in the middle. This altar included candles, stones, feathers, drums, and pieces of paper to write your intention or question for the ceremony. I wrote on the paper that I wanted clarity of purpose as I embarked on my seminary experience.

We went on three non-medicinal journeys (meaning non-plant-based medicine) led by a shamanic practitioner. The shaman led the journeys after the opening invocation, introductions, and readings from the Mayan calendar. Each person lay on the floor while his assistant drummed, and the shaman blew incense and guided us in three visualization experiences. In the first visualization, we found our grounding location where we would start all journeys. My grounding location was deep in the forest.

During the second visualization, we were asked to partner up, and in the guided meditation, we were to receive the spirit guide for our partner. My partner was to follow her intuitive knowing while putting her hands on my head and arm to feel my energy as she was being guided by the shaman leading the journey through the drumming. My partner gave me the spider as my spirit guide, which signifies feminine energy, artistry and creativity, patience, balance, and interconnection. In our third visualization, we were guided to listen to the wisdom of our spirit guide to share with us what we needed to hear for our individual journey.

As we engaged in the third shamanic vision, I found myself in the forest but quickly moved to an open field where I saw myself walking up the side of a mountain. About a quarter of the way up the mountain, I struggled to climb as I tripped and fell to the top. About halfway up the mountain, as I continued falling up the hill, I transformed into a boy around four or five years old. From this point, I started to run, skip, and jump up the mountain effortlessly. I was joyful, happy, and giggling up the side of the hill without any struggles or falls.

When I reached the top of the mountain, I walked over to the ledge and looked down. What I saw shocked me. I witnessed thousands of men crammed together in this giant pit. As I looked down, I waved my arm and said, "Hey, come up here and follow me." I'm unsure how they escaped the pit; this was a shamanic vision, so conventional physics did not apply. However, the next thing I knew, a group of men over a thousand deep walked out of the pit and toward the mountain along this wide-open field.

At a certain point, I looked back, and the men were in a single-file line following me down this path along the side of the mountain. As we continued walking, I told the men to hold hands and led them down the trail. After some time, we came across this vast spiderweb. We knew we had to walk into the web, as there was no other way to get around, and we continued in a single-file line. As each man's foot touched the web, he became a boy. We started to laugh and giggle as we continued to walk along the web.

Out of nowhere, these giant black widows started crawling toward us, but somehow, we knew not to run and to keep walking. Passing by the black widows, one of the spiders injected each boy with feminine energy. Each boy would then walk another couple of steps, and a part of him (his shadow) would die and float away. A few more steps, and he'd transform back into a man. But this time, he had this look of freedom, happiness, and joy on his face that he didn't have before. Each man also knew what he was meant to do in the world. It was like they had been liberated by an injection of feminine energy from the spider, a source of healing for men.

I've often thought about this vision and shared it in many men's circles and with many men's work leaders. What's most significant to me is the power of feminine energy through the spider's injection that offered a powerful, healing medicine for men. By reconnecting with childlike wonder, men have newfound permission to revisit their innocence and connect with key dimensions of themselves they've suppressed or rejected. As men tap into the feminine healing energy in their youthful innocence, they begin to have greater access to their curiosity, play, full emotional and creative expression, empathy, compassion, and the ability to love unconditionally through authentic connection.

Over the years, I've heard many men say they aren't creative. Many men have lost touch with their creativity and have suppressed their ability to play. I was talking with a leader once for a well-known animation company, and I mentioned that part of the work of men's healing is rediscovering play. He responded, "Yes, the men in our company are kids at heart." That can be said for most, if not all, men, but so many men don't feel they have permission to play as they act professionally and responsibly. Yet when men rediscover and allow themselves to play, they unlock their creativity in new ways and solve problems differently.

Project Compassion: Deepening Compassion in Police Departments

The day after I completed my minister's manual, the second-year culminating project, I made the decision to move from Spanish Harlem in New York City to West Asheville, North Carolina—about a month before graduating from seminary. Two days after saying my vows as an interfaith minister, I received a video from a friend.

It was the chief of police of the Asheville Police Department asking for community members to be part of police reform efforts in Asheville. In seminary, we were taught that when you hear the call, you say yes, no matter what, especially if you don't feel qualified. As I shared in the introduction, I responded the following day when I emailed him directly. By saying yes to his request, the doors with police continued to open.

From that ask, the universe brought six incredible humans together. Our group included former FBI agents, the former head of the FBI National Academy at Quantico, police and military officers, and culture transformation and masculinity experts. Over three months, we would form Project Compassion, a national initiative to deepen compassion in police departments and state/federal law enforcement agencies. Our team crosses gender, racial, sexuality, and political lines to reflect the officers and communities we serve.

I distinctly remember a conversation with a member of our team who led the FBI National Academy. As I shared my story and ideas with him, many of which are in this book, he replied, "Sean, I can't argue, rebut, or refute anything you've said. You're not talking about training cops to be better cops. You are talking about developing officers into better humans. Who can argue with that?"

We started our initiative in Chicago with a "Compassion in Policing" program for the Cook County Sheriff's corrections officers at Cook County Jail. We had total engagement from every officer in the room within fifteen minutes of the program's start. At this point, we knew we were onto something. We were tapping into the heart of some of the biggest challenges surrounding officer well-being, performance, and resilience.

A few weeks ago, we aligned with the 30x30 Initiative, an NYU Policing Project and DOJ-sponsored initiative to integrate compassion into gender equity in policing efforts—with a goal of raising the number of women in policing to 30 percent by 2030. Over two hundred and fifty police departments and five federal agencies have already signed the pledge, including the police department in Philadelphia, where I live.

Warrior Compassion: Unleashing the Healing Power of Men

Today, I am committed to creating cultures of compassion in hypermasculine systems. As I think about the success measures for my work, I ask how I can support men to deepen their level of empathy and compassion as they navigate the shifting rules, roles, and expectations around manhood, masculinity, gender, and power. Many men I speak with express feeling lost and frustrated amid these shifts. The key is to help men adapt to these changes in the world without emasculating them in the process.

This journey led to three moves in two and a half years from NYC to Asheville to Washington, DC, and landing in Philadelphia. We are focusing our compassion on policing efforts in Chicago and Philadelphia. If we can make headway in these two cities, we can reach the rest of America. These efforts will form a new compassion-centered systems change model that creates the foundation for a global compassionate healing movement reaching millions.

Reflections of a Soul Adventure

My soul adventure began when I left a successful consulting career on Wall Street and said yes to EF. I learned to relax my ego, surrender to the unknown, and walk from a place of curiosity and wonderment. Each step of my journey required me to trust the process, let go of the need to control the outcome, and follow my intuition.

Now, I'd like you to think about your journey. First, take a moment to reflect on the fact that you've been on one your entire life with many twists and turns that have led you to where you are today. Take some time to reflect on the following questions.

As you think about your journey, I ask you to consider the following:

- What aspects of my journey resonate for you as you think about your journey?
- What are you curious to explore deeper after reading about my journey over these two chapters?
- What are your thoughts and reactions to this idea of a soul adventure?
- What turns you off or raises your anxiety about a soul adventure?
- What would you want to experience on your soul adventure?
- How do you believe going on a soul adventure could change your life?

Reflecting on my soul adventure, I have walked a transformative path of self-discovery and growth. It has been a journey of surrendering to the call, stepping outside my comfort zone, and embracing the unknown with unwavering determination. A soul adventure is a quest to connect with the essence of one's being, purpose, and truth. Through seminary, shamanic journeys, and my work with Project Compassion, I have deepened my understanding of soul healing, the power of feminine energy, and the importance of compassion in hypermasculine systems. My commitment now is to create cultures of compassion and unleash the healing power of men. As I reflect on my journey, I invite you to contemplate your own path and consider the possibilities of embarking on a soul adventure.

PART III

UNLOCKING THE HEALING

———

Men's Blessing for the Soul's Journey

—SEAN HARVEY, INTERFAITH AND
INTERSPIRITUAL MINISTER

Divine Spirit, we come to you with extended arms, open
hearts, and yearning spirits.

We ask you to bless us as we begin to walk the path of our
soul's journey.

We ask you to let your light shine into our hearts to
illuminate our path.

And guide the path that each of us is called to walk as we
navigate with our sacred compass.

We are grateful for being introduced to a journey where we
unearth our inherent gifts.

Let our true divine nature surface, allowing our shy souls
to come out to play.

Walk with us at each step of the journey as new insights
help us discover our truth.

CHAPTER 5

PREPARE FOR YOUR HEALING JOURNEY

———

Three of my greatest teachers have been rabbits, rivers, and mountains on this journey. They have helped me prepare and ground for the healing journey. As a rabbit educator and bunny dad, I've deepened my comfort level in the silence and my ability to read the energy of prey animals. As a volunteer with the rabbit rescue in NYC, I was called a rabbit whisperer more than once as I could calm my energy to connect with the rabbits in ways where they would relax and purr when I picked them up. On one Christmas Eve, I was volunteering at the shelter, feeding and cleaning the cages of twenty-five rabbits. The comfort in the silence and the calm energy in the room were palpable and memorable. The ability to sit in the calm of the silence is essential for the journey.

One of my greatest loves in life is whitewater rafting. My first rafting trip was on the New and Gauley Rivers in West Virginia over twenty-five years ago. Since that time, I've rafted white water rivers on three continents, and most recently, I rafted for eight days down the Colorado River in the Grand Canyon. Whitewater rafting has been my adventure of choice for over two decades, and it reminds me to surrender my control whenever I'm on the water. Once I accepted the water was in control, I learned to surrender to it and ride the rapids.

While I lived in Asheville, I spent a lot of time on the French Broad River, the second-oldest river in the world. I would stand next to the river and tap into its ancient wisdom when contemplating and making sense of the mystery of the journey. When I needed to clear my head or let my mind wander, I would jump in the car and drive to the mountains. I found that I meditate the best while driving through the mountains. I'd often go for two to four hours at a time and often ended up in Tennessee or South Carolina. This was where I would think deeply, expansively, and creatively.

These were early practices that helped me ground and get centered. They were instrumental to my journey and continue to be as I walk my healing path. I can't emphasize this enough: the healing journey is not a quick-fix experience but a long process of evolution. For many, it can last a lifetime. From my conversations with men who have been on a healing journey, they all tell me they never consider themselves healed but instead are continually healing. As certain wounds heal, others will inevitably show up at different points in the journey. Some men have described the experience as a game of Whac-A-Mole, where they never knew where an unhealed wound might appear. In twelve-step recovery programs, it's often called "peeling back the onion."

The healing journey can be a painful experience because it requires you to face painful wounds that haven't been resolved. Many men experience the core wounding early in life but haven't had the coping tools to work through and heal them. Before engaging in the healing journey, men must be ready to engage in a long-term process. To help prepare for the journey, I outline six ways to ground as they walk into the unknown. These grounding tools are essential because they can provide a sense of stability and safety, as the healing journey can be unsettling and disorienting, where the world you know begins to shift in unfamiliar ways.

Michael Singer, a spiritual and meditation author and journalist, talks about the healing journey in this way: "If you want to be happy, you have to let go of the part of you that wants to create melodrama. This is the part that thinks there's a reason not to be happy. You have to transcend the personal, and as you do, you will naturally awaken to the higher aspects of your being. In the end, enjoying life's experiences is the only rational thing to do. You're sitting on a planet spinning around in the middle of absolutely nowhere. Go ahead, take a look at reality" (Singer 2007).

Embrace Vulnerability

One of the most transformative aspects of the men's healing journey is embracing vulnerability. Vulnerability is often seen as a sign of weakness in traditional masculine norms, leading many men to suppress their emotions and guard themselves against vulnerability. However, true healing and growth require men to courageously embrace vulnerability as a path to authenticity, connection, and emotional well-being.

When men are vulnerable, they create space for emotional honesty and authentic expression. This vulnerability invites them to acknowledge and explore their emotions, fears, and wounds without judgment or shame. By opening to vulnerability, men can access a deeper self-awareness and develop a greater capacity for empathy and compassion toward themselves and others.

Vulnerability also fosters genuine connections and deepens relationships. When men share their vulnerabilities with trusted individuals, they create a sense of intimacy, trust, and mutual support. By allowing themselves to be seen and heard in their raw and authentic state, men create opportunities for profound emotional and relational growth. The vulnerability allows for deeper connections based on genuine understanding, empathy, and acceptance.

Furthermore, embracing vulnerability empowers men to break free from societal expectations and masks that limit their true selves. It invites them to let go of the need for perfection, control, and appearing strong, allowing them to embrace their humanity and imperfections fully. By embracing vulnerability, men create space for growth, self-acceptance, and the liberation to live in alignment with their authentic values and desires.

Brené Brown, a renowned researcher and author on vulnerability and shame, emphasizes the transformative power of vulnerability in her work. She states that vulnerability is not a sign of weakness but a courageous act that allows individuals to fully engage in life, experience true connection, and cultivate resilience (Brown 2012).

As men embrace vulnerability in their healing journey, they may encounter resistance and fear. Acknowledging these emotions and providing self-compassion and support throughout the process is essential. Men can lean on their community of men, therapy, or other supportive spaces to explore vulnerability in a safe and nonjudgmental environment.

Find Safety in a Community of Men

Finding safety in a community of men can be a vital aspect of the healing journey for many men. In this journey of self-discovery and growth, connecting with other men who have faced similar challenges and experiences provides a unique space for support, empathy, and understanding. In this community, men feel a sense of belonging and validation as they share their stories, fears, and triumphs. It creates a safe, nonjudgmental space where vulnerability can be embraced and celebrated.

Showing up fully in front of a community of men can be daunting. In writing this book, several men I spoke with expressed their fears about showing vulnerability in front of other men. I spoke with Christopher Veal, a former Marine, who runs a podcast called *The Vulnerable Man*, in which he interviews men sharing their stories of vulnerability. It was clear from my conversations with Christopher and many other men I had interviewed that conditioning prevented men from truly being vulnerable. The messages that men must be strong, not show weakness, and not talk about feelings contribute significantly to the ways many men have internalized not being "allowed" to express vulnerability (Veal 2022).

In this community, men create a space where they can be accepted without judgment from other men. The type of safety that makes it ok to ugly cry in front of each other as a normal part of the journey. In these spaces, the men can learn from one another's experiences and gain valuable insights that contribute to their healing and growth. Men connecting in a community of men can break down this idea of terminal uniqueness, where they might feel like they are the only man experiencing a particular type of challenge or situation. They realize they are not alone in their struggles and don't have to face the challenges alone.

They can witness the journeys of others, finding inspiration and hope in the stories of each other's resilience and transformation. By sharing their struggles and successes, men receive support and become sources of inspiration and encouragement for their fellow men. The collective wisdom and diverse perspectives within the community help expand their understanding of themselves and the healing process.

Finding a community of men also fosters a sense of collective healing and social change. As men come together to support one another, they can challenge societal norms and stereotypes that perpetuate harmful ideals of masculinity. They create a space for men to experiment with intimacy and deepen their connection with men while breaking down feelings of fear, resentment, shame, comparison/competition, and inadequacy.

At the same time, they can understand that wounding is a normal part of the human experience and that the emotions associated with the wounds are real. The community becomes a space for redefining what it means to be a man, emphasizing values of compassion, vulnerability, and healthy masculinity. Ultimately, the men receive validation from others for who they are in their authenticity rather than how they project to be. It begins to create a different level of intimacy among men.

Building a solid and nurturing community of men who create a brave environment to get honest with each other, hold space for the emotions that come up, and provide accountability for each other is a key ingredient to support men as they start and walk their healing journeys. The antidote to the fear so many men have of other men is to learn new ways to connect on a deeper level. The deep friendships and bonds men can have and demonstrate for each other will be critical for men to learn to love themselves and start seeing the world through a lens of love rather than fear, hate, judgment, or sadness. The love men can give each other can offer other men hope, possibility, and inspiration.

See the World with Childlike Wonder

Rediscovering the ability to see the world with childlike wonder is a transformative aspect of the men's healing journey. It involves reconnecting with the curiosity, awe, and openness that often diminishes as we grow older and face life's challenges. By embracing a childlike perspective, men can approach their experiences with fresh eyes and an innate sense of wonderment. This shift in perception allows them to break free from limiting beliefs and preconceived notions, opening new possibilities for growth and healing.

Seeing the world with childlike wonder encourages men to cultivate a sense of presence and mindfulness. It invites them to fully engage with their surroundings while immersing themselves in the beauty and magic of the present moment. In this state of mind, men can experience a deep appreciation for the simple joys of life, finding awe in the natural world, connecting with others on a profound level, and rekindling a sense of playfulness and spontaneity.

Embracing a childlike perspective also invites men to explore their creativity and imagination. It encourages them to tap into their inner child and explore artistic expression through painting, writing, music, dance, or other creative outlets. Engaging in these activities allows men to unlock a wellspring of inspiration and self-expression. By embracing their creative impulses, men can discover new facets of themselves, express their emotions, and find healing through artistic exploration.

One of my mentors, Nadia Chaney, shared this insight at the creative facilitation training in Kingston, Ontario:

> "Creativity is a doorway to the inner life. It can open us up to our deeper truth."

Seeing the world with childlike wonder and creativity fosters a deeper connection with men and their inner selves. It encourages them to listen to their intuition, trust their instincts, and honor their inner guidance. By tapping into this childlike sense of inner wisdom, men can make decisions aligned with their authentic selves and find greater clarity and purpose. It becomes a powerful tool for self-discovery, self-acceptance, and personal transformation.

Incorporating the element of childlike wonder into the men's healing journey invites men to approach life with a renewed sense of curiosity, awe, and joy. It offers a path of rediscovery, self-expression, and connection to the world around them. Through the lens of childlike wonder, men embark on a transformative journey of healing, growth, and reclaiming the innate magic and joy that resides within them.

Rediscovering the creativity and play of childlike wonder also helps men let their guard down, surrender control, and let go of the need to perform. In many conversations with men, I've found that letting go can mean men will lower their guard or mask, become less self-conscious of how they look or come across to others, take themselves less seriously, and have access to their inner life.

By engaging in more creativity, play, and fun, men tend to get out of their heads and left-brain thinking and tap into their hearts, intuition, and creative minds. By connecting to our playful inner child and cultivating a sense of wonder and curiosity, we can find greater meaning and purpose in life and live more fulfilling and authentic lives.

Activate Curiosity

Curiosity is essential to any man's healing journey, as it opens doors to new possibilities, expands perspectives, and invites a sense of wonder into his life. When men cultivate curiosity, they approach life with a childlike openness, eager to explore and learn from the world around them. By embracing curiosity, men embark on a transformative path of self-discovery, allowing them to break free from stagnant patterns and embrace the fullness of their potential.

Curiosity encourages men to question, challenge assumptions, and seek more profound understanding. It invites them to explore their beliefs, emotions, and experiences with genuine interest and nonjudgment. Through curiosity, men can develop greater self-awareness and emotional intelligence, empowering them to navigate their inner landscape with compassion and clarity.

In the men's healing journey, activating curiosity invites a shift from a fixed to a growth mindset. It encourages men to embrace uncertainty, be open to different perspectives, and approach challenges with curiosity rather than fear. By cultivating curiosity, men can dismantle limiting beliefs and expand their worldview, fostering personal growth and resilience and embracing the richness and complexity of life's journey with a sense of awe and curiosity.

Surrender into the Unknown

Surrendering into the unknown is a profound aspect of the men's healing journey, inviting them into the dance of the ego, which I describe as the need for control and permission to let go. It is an act of trust and vulnerability, allowing oneself to relinquish preconceived notions, expectations, and attachments. By surrendering, men create space for new possibilities, allowing the healing process to unfold mysteriously in transformative ways.

Relaxing the ego and surrendering to the unknown involves recognizing the limitations of the ego's desire for control and the illusion of certainty. It invites men to embrace the uncertainty of life, acknowledging the forces and circumstances beyond their control. By surrendering, men release the burden of constantly trying to manage and manipulate outcomes, freeing themselves from the anxiety and stress that often accompany the need for control.

Surrendering to the unknown is not a passive act but an active choice to flow with life's currents rather than resist them. It requires cultivating a sense of trust in the unfolding of the journey, even in the face of discomfort and uncertainty. Surrendering allows men to tap into their inner strength, resilience, and adaptability, as they navigate the unpredictable terrain of life's challenges. It opens the door to new experiences, insights, and growth that may not have been possible when held tightly to the need for control.

In surrendering to the unknown, men can find liberation from the constraints of the ego and the limitations of the mind. They open themselves to the wisdom and guidance of their inner selves, intuition, and the greater universal intelligence. By relinquishing the need to know all the answers and surrendering to the flow of life, men can experience a profound sense of freedom, peace, and alignment with their true selves. Surrender becomes an invitation to embrace the mystery of life and trust in the universe's inherent wisdom.

The river has always been a powerful metaphor for my work with men and my own personal growth. As I shared earlier, whitewater rafting and kayaking are my great loves. They require this type of surrender as the river is in control, and I've had to learn to move and flow with the rapids. I've found this metaphor helpful in understanding the dance of the ego.

As men surrender into the unknown, they embark on a courageous and transformative journey of healing and self-discovery. They learn to relax the ego's grip on control, cultivate trust in the unfolding of life, and embrace the vast possibilities that arise from surrender. By surrendering, men open themselves to a deeper connection with their true essence, a greater sense of peace, and a more authentic and fulfilling life. In surrender, men find liberation, growth, and the freedom to embrace the present moment fully.

According to Michael Singer, author of *The Untethered Soul:*

> "True liberation and freedom come from surrendering to the guidance of the soul. By letting go of resistance, fears, and attachments, individuals can open themselves up to the wisdom and guidance of the soul, leading to a more fulfilling and authentic life" (Singer 2007).

By surrendering to the wisdom and guidance of the soul, men align themselves with their true essence and purpose. They tap into an inner reservoir of strength, clarity, and intuition, serving as an inner compass for navigating life's challenges and obstacles. In this state of surrender, men can experience a profound sense of liberation and freedom, as they no longer define themselves solely by external circumstances or ego demands. Instead, they find fulfillment and authenticity in living from a place of soul-inspired truth.

Listen to the Voice Within

Learning to listen to the voice within is a vital aspect of the men's healing journey, as it allows them to tap into their intuition, inner wisdom, and authentic self. In a world filled with external noise and distractions, cultivating the ability to quiet the mind and attune to one's inner voice is a transformative practice.

When men learn to listen to the voice within, they gain access to their deepest desires, values, and needs. Through this inner connection, they can make aligned choices, find clarity in decision-making, and navigate life with greater purpose and authenticity. By tuning into the voice within, men can develop a profound self-awareness and a deep understanding of their emotions, thoughts, and desires.

Listening to the voice within also opens the door to self-compassion and self-acceptance. Men often carry societal expectations and conditioning that may suppress their authentic voice. By cultivating the practice of listening to the voice within, men can honor their truth, validate their experiences, and offer themselves kindness and understanding.

This inner dialogue promotes self-love, fosters emotional healing, and nurtures a strong sense of self-worth.

Listening to the voice within is a process of reconnecting with one's intuition, inner guidance, and authentic self-expression. It involves creating space for quiet reflection, introspection, and mindfulness practices that help cultivate a deeper connection with the inner world. By developing this skill, men can access their inherent wisdom, align with their purpose, and live in alignment with their most authentic selves.

As men learn to listen to the voice within, they unlock a powerful source of inner guidance, strength, and clarity. This practice empowers them to make choices that align with their authentic values, passions, and aspirations. Ultimately, men can cultivate a deep sense of self-trust and navigate their lives.

As you think about your journey, I ask you to consider the following:

- What allows you to be more vulnerable and authentic in a community of men?
- In what ways do you allow yourself to play and express your creativity?
- How do you currently relax the ego and release your need for control?
- What emotions are stirred when you think about surrendering to the unknown?
- What have you experienced when you allowed yourself to surrender to the unknown?

The journey of healing and growth for men is a transformative and courageous path that requires embracing vulnerability, curiosity, surrender, and self-listening. By finding a community of men who provide support, empathy, and acceptance, men create a safe space for authentic expression and connection. Rediscovering the childlike wonder allows men to approach life with openness and joy while igniting curiosity opens doors to new possibilities and expands their perspectives. Surrendering into the unknown frees men from the need for control and allows for profound growth and transformation. And finally, learning to listen to the voice within provides access to inner wisdom, self-compassion, and alignment with one's authentic self. Through these practices, men embark on a profound journey of healing, self-discovery, and the reclamation of their true essence.

CHAPTER 6

BEGIN THE JOURNEY AS AN INQUIRY

———

Throughout my life, I have been that guy who was fascinated by meaning-of-life questions. Some of my closest friends have called me the philosopher. So, it wasn't surprising that I chose existential psychotherapy as my theoretical orientation for my graduate degree in counseling; I have always tried to create meaning around what I was experiencing, especially in my struggles and hardships.

Throughout my career, I've found myself helping others find their purpose. As I deepened in my journey, the work deepened. What began as assisting others to discover their career purpose evolved into helping others find their life purpose and eventually transformed into discovering their soul's purpose. However, asking the existential questions stayed consistent across the journey and were the gateway to an inner knowing, calling, and truth.

Ask the Existential Questions

In the depths of our being, beneath the layers of societal conditioning and the noise of daily life, lay profound questions that stir our souls and challenge our understanding of existence. These existential questions, often whispered in moments of contemplation, can ignite a transformative journey of self-discovery that helps us make meaning of the world and our place in it.

They ask us to explore the mysteries of life, grapple with our purpose, and seek a deeper understanding of our place in the universe. They also ask us how to love and, in turn, to define the meaning of love. The existential questions allow us to look within from a place of rigorous honesty as we unearth and discover our truth.

Asking existential questions is essential for everyone, including men, because it helps us understand our place in the world, the meaning of our lives, and our purpose. These questions help us reflect on our beliefs, values, and assumptions, leading to personal growth and development.

Men benefit from asking existential questions because they may have been socialized to suppress their emotions and focus on achievements and external success. By reflecting on more profound questions about their purpose and meaning, men can develop a more holistic understanding of themselves and their lives by looking inward and moving from the extrinsic (externally focused) to intrinsic (internally focused) motivations of their needs, wants, and desires.

Asking existential questions is an essential part of the human experience and can help men to develop a deeper understanding of themselves and the world around them. Existential questions are fundamental questions about the meaning and purpose of life, and they are often related to the nature of existence, identity, and human relationships. Here is a deeper explanation of the four existential questions at the root of my inquiry:

- **Who am I?**
  This question asks about the nature of the authentic self and our identity. It involves exploring our personality, beliefs, values, social roles, and the factors shaping our sense of self. Answering this question can involve a journey of self-discovery, reflection, and personal growth, as we explore our innermost thoughts, feelings, and desires and seek to understand our place in the world.

- **Why am I here?**
  This question asks about the purpose and meaning of our lives. It involves exploring our values, aspirations, and goals, as well as our relationships with others and our place in the larger world. Answering this question can involve a process of reflection and introspection as we seek to understand what motivates and inspires us and what gives our lives a sense of purpose and direction.

- **What am I here to do?**
  This question asks about our life's work and the impact we are meant to have on the world. It involves exploring our inherent talents, skills, and passions, as well as our values and sense of purpose. Answering this question can involve a process of reflection, experimentation, and personal growth, as we seek to find ways to align our work and passions and make a meaningful contribution to the world around us.

- **How do I love?**

  This question asks about our capacity for connection, compassion, and ability to form meaningful relationships with others. It involves exploring our emotions, attitudes, beliefs about love and relationships, and our ability to empathize with and care for others. Answering this question can involve a process of self-reflection and personal growth as we seek to deepen our capacity for connection, empathy, and compassion and cultivate more fulfilling and authentic relationships with others.

These questions are often deeply personal and challenging to answer, as they require us to confront some of the most profound mysteries of existence. By exploring these questions through reflection, conversation, or creative expression, we can create a greater sense of meaning, purpose, and connection with the world around us.

By exploring these questions, one may understand their unique gifts and talents and how they can contribute to the world, leading to a sense of spiritual purpose. Exploring these questions can inspire creativity and artistic expression. By contemplating questions about the nature of reality and the meaning of life, one may be inspired to create works of art that explore these themes, deepening their spiritual understanding.

Viktor Frankl, an Austrian psychiatrist and Holocaust survivor, explored existential questions extensively in his seminal work *Man's Search for Meaning*. In his book, Frankl reflects on his experiences in Nazi concentration camps and offers profound insights into the search for meaning in life (Frankl 1963).

Frankl emphasizes the importance of finding meaning in suffering and adversity. He argues that while individuals cannot always control their circumstances, they can choose their attitude toward those circumstances. According to Frankl, the freedom to choose one's attitude is fundamental to human existence.

Frankl asserts that finding meaning is a central motivation for human beings. He suggests that meaning can be discovered in three main ways: engaging in meaningful work or creative activities, experiencing deep connections with others through love and relationships, and finding meaning in the attitude one adopts toward unavoidable suffering.

Existential questions often touch on spiritual and philosophical issues, such as the meaning of life, the nature of consciousness, and the existence of a higher power. Embarking on an existential inquiry can lead to a deeper examination of one's beliefs about the nature of reality, the purpose of life, and divine influence and inspiration. By exploring these beliefs, one can better understand their spiritual values and how they relate to the larger world. Existential questions often lead to discussions about the nature of human existence and our place in the world. These discussions can foster a sense of community and shared values, deepening one's spiritual connections with others.

Find Truth in Nature

Finding truth in nature is a powerful and transformative aspect of a man's healing journey. Nature offers a profound connection and reflection of life's natural rhythms and cycles. As men immerse themselves in the beauty and serenity of the natural world, they tap into a deeper sense of presence, peace, and harmony. Nature becomes a teacher and guide, offering valuable insights, wisdom, and healing.

In nature, men find solace and refuge from the noise and demands of everyday life. They witness the intricate interplay of elements, the resilience of plants and animals, and the natural world's vastness. This immersion in nature's abundance and resilience reminds men of their innate capacity for strength, resilience, and adaptability. It provides a powerful reminder that they are part of something more significant, interconnected, and meaningful.

Nature also serves as a mirror, reflecting men to their inner landscape and offering moments of profound self-reflection. As men observe the cycles of growth, change, and transformation in nature, they recognize the parallels within themselves. Nature invites men to embrace impermanence, let go of attachments, and surrender to the inherent flow of life. In the stillness of nature, men can find answers to their most profound questions, clarity amid confusion, and a renewed sense of purpose and direction.

Through their connection with nature, men discover a profound sense of awe, wonder, and reverence for the natural world. They experience a deep understanding of interconnectedness with all living beings and gain a renewed appreciation for the delicate balance of ecosystems. This connection to nature sparks a desire to protect and preserve the environment, fostering a greater sense of responsibility and stewardship. Finding truth in nature ultimately catalyzes personal healing, self-discovery, and a deeper connection with the world around them.

Explore the Power of Psychedelics

In my interviews with men, over 50 percent of those I spoke with openly shared about their psychedelic experiences as part of their healing or spiritual awakening journeys. Many described their experiences as life changing and transformational. As psychedelics continue to become more mainstream, I knew I'd be remiss if I didn't mention it as a possible medicine or path along the journey for healing and expanding consciousness.

In psychedelics and plant-based medicine, men embark on a transformative inner journey that can bring about profound shifts in perception, consciousness, and self-awareness. These medicines have been used for centuries in various cultures for their therapeutic and spiritual properties. By working with psychedelics and plant-based medicine in a supportive and intentional setting, men can access heightened states of consciousness and tap into the depths of their psyche.

Psychedelics and plant medicines offer a unique opportunity for men to confront and heal past traumas, unresolved emotions, and limiting beliefs. They can provide a fresh perspective, dissolve egoic patterns, and open doors to new realms of understanding and self-compassion. These substances' altered states of consciousness allow men to access the subconscious mind, facilitating profound healing and transformation.

In the context of the men's healing journey, psychedelics and plant-based medicine can accelerate spiritual growth by expanding awareness and a profound sense of interconnectedness. They can evoke a reverence for the natural world and a renewed commitment to living in harmony with the earth. However, it is crucial to approach these substances with caution, respect, and responsible guidance, ensuring the safety and integration of the experiences into everyday life.

Michael Pollan, in his book *How to Change Your Mind: What the New Science of Psychedelics Teaches Us About Consciousness, Dying, Addiction, Depression, and Transcendence*, explores the transformative potential of psychedelics, including their impact on spiritual and soul healing. In his research and personal experiences with psychedelics, Pollan highlights the capacity of these substances to dissolve the ego and engender a sense of ego transcendence. He discusses the phenomenon of ego death and the subsequent expansion of awareness and interconnectedness that many individuals report during psychedelic experiences. According to Pollan, these ego-dissolving experiences can lead to a profound spiritual connection, often described as a merging with something greater than oneself (Pollan 2019).

Connecting with nature and exploring the realm of psychedelics and plant-based medicine offers men another path to healing, growth, and self-discovery. Through these transformative experiences, men can access profound truths, awaken their innate wisdom, and find a deep connection to themselves, others, and the natural world. Integrating these practices into the men's healing journey opens doors to profound healing, personal transformation, and a greater understanding of their place in the tapestry of life.

Follow Your Sacred Compass

As part of the men's healing journey, learning to listen to the voice within also involves following the sacred inner compass that guides them toward their true path and purpose. The sacred compass reflects the internal guidance system that aligns with their deepest values, passions, and aspirations. It is a trusted navigation tool, leading them toward a life of meaning and fulfillment.

I've tapped into my sacred compass to guide my major life decisions. While it may have given me some unexpected challenges, the ultimate outcomes have always been better than anything I could have imagined. However, those challenges were typically lessons I needed to learn to be able to refine my edges and become whole.

When I think back, in all of these decisions, I was following my sacred compass: leaving Wall Street consulting and applying to EF, attending seminary, following the call to work with men and police, writing a book, and all of the moves (Asheville, Washington, DC, and Philadelphia). When dating my current boyfriend, we knew this was the relationship we both needed at the right time.

With each move, I felt a knowing and energetic resonance as I made each decision. Energetic resonance can be described as the vibes or feelings of two or more things or people match and create a sense of connection and understanding between them. It is like being on the same wavelength with someone or something.

Following the sacred compass requires men to trust their intuition and courageously make choices that honor their authentic selves. It involves letting go of societal expectations, external validations, and the need for approval and instead embracing their inner knowing. By aligning their actions and decisions with their sacred compass, men can experience a deep sense of purpose and a profound connection to their life's journey.

When men follow their sacred compass, they embark on self-discovery and self-actualization. They tap into their unique gifts, talents, and passions and use them to contribute meaningfully to the world. By honoring their inner compass, men find the courage to step into their true power and create a life that aligns with their deepest calling and yearning.

Following the sacred compass is a transformative practice allowing men to live authentically as they walk their paths. It requires self-reflection, inner attunement, and a willingness to let go of external noise and distractions. By trusting their inner compass and following its guidance, men can navigate their lives with purpose, fulfillment, and deep internal alignment.

As you think about your journey, I ask you to consider the following:

- What existential questions do you find yourself asking the most?
- When you connect with nature, what truth and wisdom have you discovered?
- How would you describe any experiences you've had with psychedelics?
- Where is your sacred compass guiding you on the journey?
- What insights have you had from any of these practices or medicines?

In the depths of our being, existential questions beckon us to explore life's mysteries, purpose, and connection to the world around us. As men embark on a path of self-discovery, these questions become gateways to profound insights and personal growth. Reflecting on the meaning of life, our purpose, and how to love allows us to delve into the core of our existence. By immersing ourselves in nature, exploring the power of psychedelics, and following our sacred compass, we tap into the wisdom of our souls and align with our true path. Embracing these inquiries, we open ourselves to transformative and life-changing experiences. As you ponder these existential questions and explore your unique journey, may you uncover the truths that resonate within you and embark on a path of self-discovery and purpose.

CHAPTER 7

DEEPEN SPIRITUAL UNDERSTANDING

———

As an interfaith minister working with men around their healing, I often say I walk from a place of meeting men in their suffering, listening for their yearning, and offering hope in the midst of both. Throughout this book, I've shared my story where my suffering centered around my disconnection from myself and others, and my yearning has focused on creating a more profound connection. I'd been seeking a stronger relationship with my spirit and faith, with others, and within myself.

Earlier, I mentioned I became a lay leader at Marble Collegiate, my home church, where I'm a member. I first stepped into lay leadership by leading the training component for the Stephen's Ministries counseling program. I later created and led a workshop called "Being Gay and Christian," where we explored the teachings around homosexuality in the original Biblical texts.

The Biblical scholar at Marble, a Catholic nun, researched the scripture verses typically mentioned in anti-gay messaging.

She provided us with context to the deeper meanings underneath the translated messages. In her eloquence and brilliance, she dismantled each argument that spoke against homosexuality in the Bible.

Building upon her wisdom, I co-created conversations to help members of the LGBTQ+ community heal their religious trauma, examine the behaviors that were out of alignment with their core values and beliefs, and offer new ways to balance faith and sexuality in their lives. Creating this workshop was my first introduction to delving more deeply into sacred texts and offering insights into how to show up and live in today's landscape.

By studying different faith traditions in seminary (Hinduism, Buddhism, Judaism, Christianity, Islam, Sufism, Shamanism, Native American teachings, African wisdom, and integral spirituality), I began understanding the universal truths across faith traditions. Ultimately, each tradition spoke to some key ingredients for living:

- A deeper connection between oneself and a divine source.
- Being in service of others beyond ourselves.
- Holding ourselves and each other with compassion.
- Surrendering the ego and walking into the mystery.
- Experiencing a rebirth and spiritual awakening.

Virtually all spiritual and ethical systems and traditions emphasize the importance of empathy, kindness, and respect for others, and these values are often expressed through compassion. While there may be differences in how compassion is understood and practiced across different traditions, it is a fundamental human value that people of all backgrounds and beliefs share.

Even those who do not identify with a particular religion or faith tradition may recognize the importance of compassion and seek to embody this quality in their relationships and interactions with others. Ultimately, compassion is a universal human value that transcends religious and cultural boundaries, and it is an essential aspect of building a just and ethical society that prioritizes the well-being of all individuals.

Compassion is rooted in a deep connection with others and recognizes our shared humanity. It arises from an understanding that the suffering of one affects the whole and that we have a responsibility to care for and support one another. This innate quality requires us to recognize all human beings' inherent dignity and worth, regardless of their background, beliefs, or actions. Compassion asks us to tap into our shared humanity.

Compassion is about recognizing the fundamental interconnectedness of all beings and acting in ways that promote healing, justice, and human flourishing for all. Whether expressed through acts of service, charitable giving, or advocacy for social justice and human rights, compassion is a fundamental human value essential for building a just and ethical society that prioritizes the well-being of all individuals.

As I think about the many paths on the spiritual journey, I'm reflecting on a conversation with one of my closest friends, Quentin Finney. Quentin is a former Marine who went on to work for Google and now guides others around mindfulness practices for better performance. He shared, "With the true spiritual paths, they're all doors leading into the same room. We're all trying to get to the same thing. We just have different ways of trying to enter that room. Which I would call love, the place of pure love. Let's break out of the judgment that there's only a one-path mindset."

Examining Compassion across Traditions

If we take a deeper dive exploration into each of the significant spiritual and faith traditions, here are definitions of compassion reflected in some of the major traditions:

- **Christianity**
  Compassion in Christianity is the virtue of caring for others with love and mercy, following Jesus' example (Luke 6:36, NIV). It involves showing kindness, forgiveness, and selflessness to alleviate suffering and promote healing (Colossians 3:12, NIV). Christians are called to reflect God's infinite compassion in their interactions with others and fulfill the commandment to love their neighbors as themselves (Matthew 22:39, NIV).

- **Judaism**
  Compassion in Judaism, known as "Rachamim," is deeply rooted in the Torah and Jewish tradition (Gemara Yevamot 79a). It involves empathizing with the suffering of others and responding with acts of kindness and support (Deuteronomy 15:7-8, NIV). Compassion extends beyond sympathy and encompasses loving-kindness, charity, and social justice. It is seen as a moral imperative to repair and better the world (Micah 6:8, NIV).

- **Islam**
  Compassion in Islam, called "Rahma," is a central virtue emphasizing kindness, mercy, and benevolence. It involves showing empathy and concern for the suffering of others and seeking to alleviate their burdens.

Compassion extends to all of creation, promoting harmony, justice, mercy, and social welfare in society (The Qur'an 21:107).

- **Sufism**
Sufi teachings take compassion to deeper and more mystical levels, emphasizing the development of a personal connection with the Divine. Compassion in Sufism transcends ethical virtue; it becomes a transformative spiritual path. It is seen as a way to purify the heart, dissolve the ego, and unite with the Divine Beloved (Barks 2004).

- **Hinduism**
Compassion in Hinduism is expressed through the concept of "Karuna." It emphasizes empathy, understanding, and a genuine desire to alleviate the suffering of all living beings (Bhagavad Gita 6.30). Compassion is seen as a means to transcend the ego, realize one's true nature, and cultivate spiritual growth (Bhagavad Gita 12.13).

- **Buddhism**
Compassion in Buddhism, expressed as "Karuna" and practiced as loving-kindness or "Metta," involves deep empathy and a sincere wish for the well-being and liberation from the suffering of all beings. It is considered a fundamental virtue on the path to enlightenment (Karaniya Metta Sutta: The Discourse on Loving-Kindness; Sutta Nipata).

- **Shamanism**
Compassion in shamanic teachings recognizes the interconnectedness of all beings and the web of life. It

involves developing respect for nature, listening to its wisdom, and acting with empathy, balance, and reciprocity (Ingerman 1991).

- **Integral Spirituality**
  Compassion is essential for spiritual development and awakening in the integral spirituality framework. It involves recognizing interdependence, cultivating empathy, and embracing a holistic understanding of reality, including physical, psychological, and spiritual dimensions (Wilber 2007).

Exploring the Universal Truths of Compassion

Universal truths about compassion are reflected in the teachings across many different faiths and religions, from Christianity and Islam to Buddhism and Hinduism. While there may be differences in how compassion is understood and practiced across different traditions, these core principles remind us of the fundamental human value of empathy, kindness, and concern for the well-being of others and ourselves.

1. Compassion arises from recognizing our interconnectedness with others and a deep understanding that the suffering of one affects the whole.
2. Compassion involves empathy, kindness, and an active concern for the well-being of others.
3. Compassion requires us to recognize all human beings' inherent dignity and worth, regardless of their background, beliefs, or actions.

4. Compassion is expressed through action, whether through charitable giving, volunteering, or advocacy for social justice and human rights.
5. Compassion is seen as a central aspect of spiritual growth and ethical living, and it is often expressed through a range of practices that seek to cultivate a sense of connection and empathy with all beings.

Love at the Root of Compassion

Love is considered the foundation of compassion because both are rooted in a deep connection with others. Love is the recognition of our shared humanity and the desire to act in ways that promote the well-being of others. Compassion arises from this same recognition of our interconnectedness and the deep understanding that the suffering of one affects the whole. Love and compassion are complementary qualities that create a sense of connection and empathy with all beings.

As the Dalai Lama, the spiritual leader of the Tibetan people, writes, "Love and compassion are necessities, not luxuries. Without them, humanity cannot survive" (Dalai Lama 1998). Love and compassion are seen as essential aspects of spiritual growth and human flourishing, and they are often expressed through acts of service, kindness, and generosity that seek to alleviate suffering and promote well-being for all.

As an interfaith minister, I speak to the suffering and yearning of others and myself. At the same time, I subscribe to the teachings of Christ, shamanic practices and wisdom, and the mysticism of the Sufi tradition in the Islamic faith. As a spiritual leader and interfaith minister, energetically and spiritually, something beyond the human condition is critical to our healing as men and humans. Yet it comes down to the movement from disconnection, isolation, and loneliness to a deeper capacity of love, compassion, and humanity among men—from me to we to one (interconnectedness).

Deepening Spiritual Understanding

Spiritual understanding helps us see our interconnectedness and oneness and the Divine when we begin to see each other and ourselves beneath the labels and layers (titles, status, and achievements) beyond our differences and get us to our core humanity, and when we can see each other as incredible, unique, and beautiful humans who share the same core needs to be loved, to be valued, to belong, to be witnessed, to be included.

As we embrace each person, we interact from a place of love, curiosity, and compassion. This enables us to accept others' truths rather than seeing the truth from our lens exclusively, where we honor their journeys, challenges/struggles, gifts, contributions, and the joy they bring into the world.

At the essence of spiritual understanding is our ability to relax our egos and open our hearts to love to embrace each person for their unique humanity. As we learn to love ourselves and remove judgment, expectations, and shame, we begin to see ourselves in the eyes of others through the transforming power of love.

The Power of Self-Compassion and Forgiveness

Self-compassion is a fundamental aspect of our personal and interpersonal well-being. By nurturing self-compassion, we create a foundation for extending love and compassion to others. It begins with acknowledging and embracing ourselves fully, including our strengths and imperfections. Through self-compassion, we cultivate a deep sense of acceptance and understanding, allowing us to let go of self-judgment and approach ourselves with kindness and forgiveness.

As we embark on a self-compassion path, forgiveness emerges as a transformative force. Forgiveness enables us to release the burden of past hurts inflicted by ourselves and others. It involves recognizing our own shortcomings, the ways we may have hurt others, and the injuries we have suffered. By extending forgiveness, we shift our perspective from blame and resentment to compassion and empathy. We understand each person is doing their best with the tools they have, and behind every behavior lies a deeper story waiting to be understood.

We cultivate an open and compassionate heart when we transition from judging others to curiosity and acceptance. This shift allows us to see beyond surface-level actions and connect with the underlying experiences, fears, and desires that drive human behavior. By practicing forgiveness and embracing self-compassion, we embark on a path of healing and growth. The forgiveness we offer to others and ourselves is key to unlocking stuck energy, releasing underlying resentments, and fostering deep transformation within us.

In this journey of self-compassion and forgiveness, we realize loving and accepting ourselves unconditionally is the gateway to genuinely seeing others in their truth. As we let go of conditions and judgments, we open ourselves to a profound connection with others grounded in empathy and understanding. Through self-compassion, forgiveness, and an open heart, we foster a transformative power of love that ripples outward, positively impacting our relationships and creating a more compassionate and harmonious world.

Introducing Compassionate Masculinity

While in seminary, I began using the term "compassionate masculinity" to describe an ideal version of masculinity. Compassionate masculinity embodies empathy, kindness, and connection within the construct of masculinity. It challenges the notion that strength and compassion are mutually exclusive, recognizing that men can embrace both qualities. At its core, compassionate masculinity acknowledges the interconnectedness of all living beings and aspires to create a more just and sustainable world for everyone.

Compassionate masculinity recognizes all beings' inherent worth and dignity, fostering respect and care for others. Rather than perpetuating a sense of separateness and disconnection, compassionate masculinity encourages men to embrace their shared humanity with others. It rejects harmful behaviors such as violence, aggression, and exploitation often associated with traditional masculine norms. It invites men to challenge societal norms and redefine what it means to be a man in a more inclusive, caring, and supportive way.

Empathy, connection, and vulnerability are celebrated in this vision of masculinity. Self-care and wellness play a crucial role in cultivating compassionate masculinity. Men are encouraged to acknowledge and honor their emotions, foster meaningful relationships, and act as bridge builders and changemakers to help create a more compassionate world.

A deepened spiritual understanding provides a framework for men to connect with their inner selves, cultivate self-awareness, and develop a deep sense of compassion. This spiritual connection also supports men in healing and transforming the wounds and conditioning that may have hindered their ability to express compassion. It invites them to embrace their own emotions and vulnerabilities.

Elevating compassionate masculinity is not an easy task, but it is necessary. As men continue to work toward this goal, they will not only benefit themselves. The spiritual connection to compassionate masculinity encourages men to lead with integrity, authenticity, and commitment to service. Compassionate masculinity encourages men to use their power and influence to benefit others and contribute to the greater good. Ultimately empowering them to play a vital role in building a more peaceful and sustainable world for future generations.

As you think about your journey, I ask you to consider the following:

- What resonates for you based on the definitions of compassion through the various faith traditions?
- How do you define compassion for yourself?
- How does deepening your spiritual understanding help anchor you in the ways you express compassion?
- How do you practice self-compassion and forgiveness in your life?
- How do you embody compassionate masculinity as a man?
- What's possible in your world when you deepen the level of compassion and love in your life?

Deepening our understanding of compassion is a transformative journey that transcends religious and cultural boundaries. It is a universal human value that calls us to recognize our interconnectedness and to extend kindness, empathy, and care to all beings. Through the teachings of various faith traditions, such as Buddhism, Christianity, Islam, Sufism, Judaism, and Shamanism, we learn compassion is not merely a theoretical concept but a lived practice that can bring healing and transformation to ourselves and the world. As we embody compassion daily, embracing self-compassion, forgiveness, and a vision of compassionate masculinity, we build a more loving, just, and interconnected world for all. Our journeys into deepening compassion and spiritual understanding can lead us to a deeper understanding of ourselves, others, and the profound power of love.

PART IV

UNBLOCKING
THE WOUNDS

———

A Man's Prayer for Love and Connection

A Prayer to Aphrodite on Behalf of All Men

—SEAN HARVEY, INTERFAITH AND
INTERSPIRITUAL MINISTER

Goddess of love, passion, and grace, what can you teach men about love?

What becomes possible when we can access your full feminine expression of love, desire, and connection?

Share with men your wisdom and guidance to access the full transforming power of love.

Let the light of your love shine on each man so that he can feel your healing and transforming power.

Break down the walls that inhibit our hearts from expressing freely and connecting deeply.

Remove the shame and guilt of sexuality and the fear of love and intimacy that inhibits us as men.

Show us how love becomes the life force for our full emotional and creative expression.

Help us untether love, sex, and intimacy in healthy, fulfilling ways that make us whole.

Bring us to a place of open-heartedness, compassion, and
    deeper connection in our full expression of love and in
    all of our relationships.

Let the full expression of men's access to love bring light
    and healing to all women, and the relationships between
    men and women be forever healed.

Create new possibilities in healing the world when love
    is the life force illuminating men and women as they live
    into their full expression and embrace the transforming
    power of love.

CHAPTER 8

UNEARTH THE DEEPER WOUNDS

EF focused its learning initiatives on personal transformation work, which differs from most other companies' traditional learning and development. Eileen believed if employees were allowed to engage in personal transformation experiences to become more integrated and whole, they would become better employees. In her eyes, this is good business sense.

At the heart of personal transformation lies the recognition that growth and healing are rooted in self-compassion. By embracing our wounds, unmet needs, and limiting beliefs, we can access the transformative power of love—for ourselves and for others. This journey toward self-compassion begins with an understanding that love starts from within and extends to how we care for ourselves, show compassion for others, and offer forgiveness.

By accepting and embracing our whole selves, including the aspects we perceive as imperfect or flawed, we can cultivate deeper self-love and extend that love to others. This process of self-discovery and healing allows us to see others in their truth, free from judgment or conditions. It opens the door to authentic connections and a more compassionate world.

Understanding Our Deeper Wounds

Wounds are emotional or psychological injuries from painful experiences, traumas, or unresolved conflicts. These wounds can manifest on various levels, including the physical, emotional, mental, and spiritual aspects of a person's being. Multiple factors, such as childhood trauma, abusive relationships, loss, neglect, or societal pressures, can cause wounds.

Emotional wounds often impact individuals, affecting their thoughts, emotions, beliefs, and behaviors. They can create deep-seated pain, fear, and insecurity, leading to patterns of self-sabotage, self-limitation, and difficulty in forming healthy relationships. Wounds can also contribute to developing defense mechanisms, such as denial, avoidance, or emotional numbing, to protect oneself from further pain.

Healing wounds often involves exploring and processing emotions, revisiting past experiences, challenging limiting beliefs, and developing healthy coping mechanisms. This is particularly salient for men, who typically engage in healing and transformation work at a lower rate than women. This isn't a new insight, as men in the men's healing movement have discussed this for years. One of the grandfathers of the men's healing movement, Robert Bly, sums it up in his book *Iron John* (Bly 1990): "Men also need to heal, not only from their wounds but from the silence that holds them in place. When they find their voice, their own way to heal, they can heal others."

It is important to note that wounds are not inherently harmful or something to be ashamed of. They are part of the human experience and can catalyze growth, self-aware-ness, and transformation. By acknowledging and addressing these wounds, men can heal, release emotional burdens, and cultivate greater resilience, self-compassion, and well-being.

At EF, we engaged in several modalities to unearth the deeper wounds. The ones that stood out the most for me included the unmet needs experience, the limiting beliefs work, the family constellation process, the sacred sculp-ture experiences, and finally, the drawing exercise piecing together our individual purpose statements.

Of these experiences, I'll share the three most helpful modalities in my journey: unearthing unmet needs, unpack-ing limiting beliefs, and understanding the shadow. Below, I'll walk through highlights from the personal transforma-tion experiences I've engaged in that helped me become more integrated when I identified and named my wounds.

Our Unmet Needs

In this experience, we identified our unmet needs as children and our reactions to not meeting those needs in our adult lives. Unmet needs can be described as unfulfilled desires and yearnings within us that shape our beliefs, behaviors, and relationships, often stemming from experiences of lack-ing love, acceptance, validation, or belonging. Ultimately this experience is helpful by examining the meaning we make in our lives today when our original unmet needs are not met.

In one of the purpose and personal transformation expe-riences, I distinctly remember about thirty-eight participants in the space. After the unmet needs exercise, each participant was asked to name their unmet need. The unmet needs fell into one of seven categories: to be loved, to be valued, to belong, to be seen, to be heard, to be welcomed, and to be respected. At that moment, I realized this work brings us into our deeper humanity and where we can see our shared humanity in each other. When we can see each other from our core fundamental needs, we can see the humanness in each other rather than how we may be divided at the surface.

Regardless of our upbringing and childhood quality, many men I've spoken with have an unmet need of not feeling like they are enough. It could be compounded by the desire to be seen, valued, or loved, but this message of not being enough is pervasive in many conversations. Many of these unmet needs lead to limiting beliefs that have defined how we live or don't live our lives—the risks we take and how we keep ourselves safe.

According to Jed Diamond, a pioneer in the men's healing movement for over fifty years, "men have unmet needs for emotional connection, intimacy, and validation that often go unacknowledged. By addressing these needs, men can experience greater fulfillment in their relationships and personal growth" (Diamond 2004).

When men can address their unmet needs, they fill the void of what has been missing in their lives. Understanding how men are activated when their core needs are unmet allows them to get to the root of their beliefs, emotions, and actions.

Our Limiting Beliefs

I was first introduced to my limiting beliefs at the Human Interaction Lab (HI Lab) I attended during my first year on the job at EF. The HI Lab is a personal growth experience focused on self-awareness, interpersonal skills, and knowledge of group dynamics. This experience is based on the principles of emotional intelligence: the ability to identify emotions (in both you and others), realize the powerful effects of those emotions, and apply that information to guide behavior.

There were thirteen people in our HI Lab, including two facilitators, and we met for about thirteen hours a day for five days. The facilitators would share some fundamental concepts each morning that served as the instruction for the day and guided the discussions. We usually had three two-hour human interaction lab sessions a day. The main ground rule for the experience focused on the group sharing what was happening in the "here and now" (in our current group dynamic in real time) rather than the "there and then" (this included theory, experiences from the past, or any references to things outside of the group dynamic).

This was my first experience with deeper personal transformation work. On the first day, we learned the basics of being in a HI Lab—where our interactions are the lab. On the second day, we learned to identify the emotions coming up based on our interactions with each other and our projects. We learned to distinguish our feelings from our thoughts and beliefs on the third day. On the fourth day, we began to examine our limiting beliefs that were coming up and the ways they were impacting our relationships with others. On the fifth day, we integrated the learning throughout the experience and reflected on the shifts we noticed in ourselves and our group dynamics.

We engaged in lectures, exercises, and group processes over five days that illustrated our beliefs about the world, people, and ourselves. We were asked to examine our negative thoughts—which were coming through the mirroring from others during the previous few days. I think the exercises themselves brought out some of the limiting beliefs. From the many conversations I've had with people over the years, I don't think many of us look at our limiting beliefs in direct ways.

I also want to make a distinction between therapy and personal transformation work. While therapy typically focuses on one-on-one dialogue with a therapist, personal transformation work introduces an experiential growth approach through facilitated experiences/conversations in the community with others. These experiences often directly examine certain situations using reflective/contemplative practices and creative exercises to help individuals develop insights about themselves.

This was my first experience when I started to tell my story to others in a public forum, which was important because I could articulate my story, hear my narrative out loud, and speak about the emotions I was experiencing. More importantly, I could see how others reacted to my story—how they received me and, more importantly, how they accepted me.

This allowed me to start challenging my own limiting beliefs of myself and to seek more data points of how I'm perceived in the eyes of others. I can't emphasize enough the power of storytelling and the ways it can transform our limiting beliefs of ourselves. It was in the limiting beliefs work that I had some new epiphanies.

Until I began doing my inner work, I walked through life believing I wasn't good enough, attractive, or intelligent. If I'm honest, I believed I was meant to be alone, and no one would ever want me as a friend or a lover. These limiting beliefs developed from trauma at a young age and years of bullying. These tapes, my demons, became my drivers in life. They drove me to get two and a half master's degrees to show that I wasn't stupid. I tried many different athletics—gymnastics, wrestling, cheerleading, dance, and even taught aerobics to fight my perception that I was too fat. And I slept with many men to get validation that I was attractive and not as ugly as I thought I was in my head.

Growing up, I also carried the tape that I wasn't man enough or masculine enough because I had some feminine qualities and was gay. It wasn't about trying to man up; it was becoming invisible because I would never be man enough. For most of my life, I stayed in the shadows because I never thought my voice mattered, that I mattered, and that I was a burden on others. Early in life, I learned to stay invisible and not draw attention to myself.

At the end of the HI Lab, I identified several limiting beliefs holding me back, and where I had the opportunity to reframe them in affirming ways that allowed me to shift my worldview. This helped me see and experience the world differently. I started to embrace the ways I was unique so my difference wasn't something to hide from or be ashamed of, but instead something to be cherished and shown to the world. This would be how I could bring healing into the world by embracing all aspects of myself.

By examining our limiting beliefs objectively, we can rewrite our scripts by replacing our limiting beliefs with affirming beliefs of who we are. Rewriting the script allows you to begin eliminating the "shoulds" and expectations placed on you and the expectations you've put on yourself based on the messages you've internalized. It starts with deeper reflection, intentionality, and practice to make the shift. Ultimately helping you move from knee-jerk reactions when activated by something that triggers your old tapes to a more thoughtful response reflecting the truth of who you are.

Our Shadow

The shadow is a Jungian concept that refers to the unconscious, often hidden aspects of our personality that we prefer not to acknowledge or accept. The shadow represents the parts of ourselves that we deem unacceptable, undesirable, or morally wrong. These aspects can include our fears, insecurities, repressed emotions, and instincts contrary to our conscious identity (Jung 1959).

I had many experiences during my journey where I could identify and work through my shadow. In working my shadow, I looked at the places where I had judgment for others—the type of judgment where I was triggered by someone in their mere presence or by certain behaviors. I was judging someone else for something I did not like in myself, or because they reminded me of someone who hurt me in the past.

We are often unaware of our shadow, which might not come out in therapy. In our interactions, we can see something in others that we often cannot see within ourselves. Now, therapy can be helpful to identify the shadow based on the stories/experiences we share with our therapist. However, the triggers and our projections are visceral in a group setting. We can feel what is happening within our bodies when we become triggered. The key to our shadow is realizing we are being triggered in real-time, feeling into our bodies, and moving from knee-jerk reactions to thoughtful responses.

One of my most potent shadow experiences occurred with Joe Laur and his wife, Sarah Schley, at their house in Western Massachusetts. I first met Sarah and Joe at EF when they were facilitating a systems-thinking exercise on sustainability efforts for the company. They are both systems-thinking consultants for socially conscious businesses. You might recall I mentioned Joe earlier as an elder in the men's healing movement and his work with ManKind Project. They both also lead shadow work experiences as part of personal growth for leaders.

I engaged in an hour-and-a-half shadow experience that blended four Jungian archetypes: warrior, lover, magician, and sovereign. At the same time, a psychodrama experience was created where "actors" in the space played different roles of people from my childhood. Psychodrama is a form of psychotherapy in which individuals act out events from their past. In this shadow experience, I had my parents, my grandparents on my mother's side, bullies from my K-12 years, and babysitters who molested me when I was a four-year-old.

During the experience, I was supported and held in a room of about fifteen people, with some playing roles in my story. In this immersive ninety-minute experience, I could go back to speak to the pain I experienced from different individuals in my account by speaking directly to the characters who hurt me. I could express the rage that led to loud screaming and ugly crying. I even threw a few punches. Individuals wore protective gear and padding to receive the punches without injury. I had the cathartic release to move from deep pain to healing.

Engaging in the shadow work, I saw parts of myself that were invisible to me for a good portion of my life. I often operated in the world, believing people hated me when they first met me. I had to heal from my relationships by learning to forgive my babysitters, parents, grandparents, and bullies. The specifics of these relationships hold less relevance to learning to deepen awareness of the shadow, see its impact, learn to forgive, and develop a new relationship with the past. Ultimately living from a place of healing over the wounding.

I engaged in a second shadow work experience at EF based on Debbie Ford's model. In her model, she introduces four concepts to support the healing and transformation journey (Ford 2010):

- **Shadow Awareness**
  Ford encourages individuals to become aware of their shadow, which consists of the suppressed, denied, or rejected aspects of their personality. This step includes exploring the dark, hidden, or disowned parts that often elicit shame, guilt, or fear.

- **Compassionate Inquiry**
  Ford advocates for approaching the shadow with compassion and nonjudgment. Instead of viewing the shadow as something to be fixed or eradicated, she encourages individuals to explore it with curiosity, understanding, and self-compassion.

- **Shadow Integration**
  Ford emphasizes the importance of integrating shadow aspects into our conscious awareness. By embracing and accepting these aspects, individuals can reclaim their power, heal inner wounds, and develop a greater sense of wholeness.

- **Personal Transformation**
  Ford sees the journey of healing the shadow as a transformative process that allows individuals to break free from self-limiting patterns and self-sabotaging

behaviors. By integrating the shadow, individuals can cultivate self-awareness, self-acceptance, and personal empowerment.

The experience helped me deepen my insight into my shadow experience, especially in the shadow awareness phase. However, it was through compassionate inquiry that I could form a new relationship with my shadow. This included understanding the causes and identifying the gifts from my pain, wounding, and shadow, which helped me integrate in a new way and begin to accept more parts of myself that I used to deny, feel shame around, or fear examining.

Robert Augustus Masters, a psychotherapist and spiritual teacher, offers valuable insights on healing men's shadow in his work. Masters emphasizes the importance of men engaging in deep self-exploration and confronting their shadow aspects to facilitate healing and personal growth. He encourages men to explore the unconscious patterns, fears, and repressed emotions that influence their thoughts, behaviors, and relationships (Masters 2018).

As I have talked to men who have engaged in their men's healing work, the work around unmet needs, limiting beliefs, and the shadow are paramount to better understanding ourselves and knowing where healing is needed. We do not reject these wounds as much as we acknowledge, honor, and reframe them so we can begin to see ourselves differently. Nevertheless, the unmet needs, the limiting beliefs, and our shadows are all operating and can keep us from seeing the truth of who we are until we begin to heal.

As you think about your journey, I ask you to consider the following:

- What's surfacing for you as you read through these types of wounds that we carry with us?
- How do your unhealed wounds show up in your life?
- How have these unhealed wounds prevented you from living your potential and desired life?
- In what ways have you acknowledged your unmet needs, reframed your limiting beliefs, or shed light on your shadow?
- What actions do you want to begin taking to heal your wounds?
- How are you holding yourself with compassion as you reflect on your wounds?

Embarking on a personal transformation journey that addresses our unmet needs, limiting beliefs, and shadow aspects can profoundly activate growth and healing. By delving into our deeper wounds and embracing the discomfort of self-reflection, we open ourselves to the possibility of realizing new potentials and becoming more authentic individuals. Recognizing that wounds are a natural part of the human experience, we can approach them with self-compassion and seek support from trusted sources to navigate our healing journey.

As we uncover and reframe our limiting beliefs, meet our unmet needs, and integrate our shadow, we can move toward greater self-awareness, resilience, and the ability to live authentically. Embracing our wounds as part of our human experience allows us to be genuine, connect with others, and make positive contributions to the world.

CHAPTER 9

EMBRACE THE SOUL-HEALING JOURNEY

I remember having a conversation with Marianne Williamson at a fundraising gala hosted by my seminary. Before this conversation, I attended one of her Tuesday evening gatherings at Marble. She would give talks every other Tuesday evening at my church. I noticed the audience was about 85 percent women and about 15 percent men. I left the gathering asking, "Where do men go for spiritual growth?"

When I talked with Marianne a year later at the gala, I asked her where men go for spiritual growth and why her audience had so few men. She responded, "Sean, that's not my challenge to figure out. This is your calling and your challenge to discover the answer. However, I can tell you that some men tell me they can't hear the message through my voice. That's why it's important that you explore this calling to support men in their spiritual growth."

Ever since that conversation, I've spent much time grappling with the question. Part of my motivation for writing this book is to offer insights and stories for men to contemplate practical spirituality in their lives and for men to be able to walk a soul-healing path that is accessible.

Perspectives from *A Course in Miracles*

Marianne Williamson is best known for her teachings using *A Course in Miracles* (ACIM). What I find most profound about ACIM is its practicality, accessibility, and deep wisdom. ACIM touches upon soul healing through four key principles (Schucman 1976):

- **Healing as a Shift in Perception**
  ACIM teaches that healing changes how we perceive ourselves and the world. It emphasizes that true healing involves letting go of ego-based thoughts, grievances, and illusions and aligning our minds with the truth of love and oneness.

- **The Power of Forgiveness**
  ACIM places a strong emphasis on forgiveness as a means of healing. It teaches that forgiveness is the key to releasing the past, letting go of grievances, and experiencing inner peace. By forgiving ourselves and others, we allow healing to occur at a deep level.

- **Recognizing the Illusion**
  ACIM views the world as a projection of the ego's fear-based thought system. It teaches that healing comes from recognizing the illusory nature of the world and shifting our identification from the ego to the truth of our divine self.

- **Awakening to the Truth**
  ACIM presents the idea that our true identity is not rooted in the body or the ego, but in the eternal, unchangeable essence of the soul. It suggests healing involves awakening to this truth and remembering our divine nature.

Defining Soul

As an interfaith minister, I'm often asked, what is soul or soulfulness? The soul is often seen as the spiritual essence of an individual that transcends religious boundaries. It is considered the core that connects with the divine and is reflected in one's highest essence or definition of self.

The soul is believed to be eternal, carrying the essence of a person's identity and consciousness beyond physical existence. Many of ACIM teachings we've touched upon in other areas of the book. However, I want to highlight the continued focus on forgiveness and how we awaken to truth.

Marianne continued our conversation around men not being able to hear the message through her even if they resonate with the teachings. She added that some men need a masculine voice to hear, digest, and internalize spiritual messages. This is our opportunity for men to support other men on the soul-healing path, where we can guide, challenge, and celebrate each other's journey; where we teach and learn from each other and delve deeper into the discovery of our own truth. To stand beside each other in the pain and struggle of the journey and simultaneously walk side by side is to know that we are never alone walking the path.

Interfaith perspectives on the soul emphasize the shared values and principles that underlie various religious and spiritual traditions. As men on the healing path, we can examine our values and come to new understandings of the ways we show up in the world and what's holding us back from coming into our full truth. At the heart of these values: love, compassion, justice, and the pursuit of spiritual growth and transformation. The soul is seen as the vehicle through which men can connect with the sacred and cultivate a deeper sense of meaning, purpose, and connection with others.

In interfaith contexts, the focus often shifts toward finding common ground and promoting understanding and respect among different beliefs and practices. Rather than seeking a single, definitive definition of the soul, interfaith perspectives encourage dialogue, learning, and appreciating the rich diversity of spiritual understandings while recognizing the interconnectedness of all beings on a shared spiritual journey. Spiritual understanding teaches us that we can see the truth in others as we discover our truth. Ultimately, we can accept both truths as true without judgment, fear, or anger. We begin to see each other in our shared humanity.

Understanding the Soul-Healing Journey

The soul-healing journey is a man's transformative path toward healing and wholeness at a deep, spiritual level. It is a process of self-discovery, self-reflection, and inner exploration to address emotional, psychological, and spiritual wounds. During this journey, men engage in various practices and modalities that support their healing, such as therapy, meditation, energy work, creative and expressive arts, and somatic practices.

The soul-healing journey involves delving into the depths of one's being, uncovering and integrating aspects of the self that have been wounded, suppressed, or forgotten. It is a sacred voyage of self-compassion, self-acceptance, and self-love, where men confront their pain, embrace their vulnerabilities, and release patterns and beliefs that no longer serve their growth and well-being. Through this transformative process, individuals can experience profound healing, reconnect with their authentic essence, and cultivate a sense of wholeness, purpose, and inner peace.

A soul-healing journey for men helps them explore their deeper humanity in ways they can hear the voice of their highest selves and their soul's calling. They begin by grappling with existential questions to understand what gives them meaning and purpose. These men can have stronger relationships by creating greater intimacy with themselves, others, and the divine. Spiritual understanding becomes a way to embrace greater acceptance of what is rather than how they've perceived the world. The ability to relax the ego shifts from judgment to curiosity and acceptance. Men on a soul-healing journey learn to love in new ways as love becomes the center of their essence and how they show up in the world.

In essence, a men's healing journey primarily focuses on addressing specific wounds and challenges men face in their personal and social lives. In contrast, a man's soul-healing journey delves into the spiritual dimensions of his being, seeking to awaken and align with his deeper soul essence and purpose. Both journeys are interconnected and can complement each other in supporting men's overall healing, growth, and self-discovery.

As you might have already gathered, the soul-healing journey is winding and circuitous. Or, as my friend Ross

Guttler, the CEO of the Open Center in New York City, says, "The path is meandering. As you're learning, you don't go back in your learning. You don't become less learned. It makes me think that definition of meandering needs to be considered differently. As you walk the path, you keep moving forward. But metaphorically, sometimes, you go through struggles and either work through the struggles or get off the path. But are you ever really off the path? Your twists and turns are the path."

As I lived by my script, I had internalized the messages that I had to be the best—the smartest, most successful, financially well off, extremely social, and above all else, hypermasculine. This led to a life of striving, checking off all the boxes, and feeling inauthentic about who I was. When I didn't live up to these standards, I felt broken. The broken feeling, combined with low self-worth, took me further into my addictive behaviors to cope and escape from the pressures and the real feelings that I was "less than" by measures and expectations I had created for myself. I couldn't even see the ways I was wounded.

It wasn't until I could forgive myself and have compassion for my "brokenness." I could start releasing my attachments to my own self-loathing. Through self-compassion and forgiveness, I started to feel liberated from the pain and constriction of all the messages, limiting beliefs, and fears driving my life. I also stopped thinking that I was broken and acknowledged that I was deeply wounded as a man.

While walking my path, I heard my soul's calling to engage in my healing work and help other men heal. As I began to walk deeper into my calling, it evolved to bringing healing into hypermasculine systems and working with men operating from hypermasculine mindsets.

Hypermasculine mindsets can be defined as an exaggerated or extreme form of masculinity often characterized by rigid adherence to traditional gender roles and expectations associated with masculinity. Men who embrace this form of masculinity may prioritize competition, power, and control while devaluing qualities traditionally associated with the feminine.

Hypermasculine systems refer to societal structures, institutions, and cultural norms that uphold and perpetuate the ideals and values of hypermasculinity. This can also include male-dominated organizations and institutions that hold onto these perceptions, expectations, and beliefs.

My level of intimacy in my relationships deepened where I could accept another's truth, even if it was diametrically opposed to mine. I could listen to the voice within as I navigated the world from my inner or sacred compass. Most notably, I shifted from a scarcity to an abundancy mindset and found that connections and opportunities opened effortlessly and seamlessly.

As I walked through the world from a place of awe and wonderment, I no longer felt trapped by my fears and insecurities. I moved through the world with confidence, curiosity, and a sense of love, allowing me to maneuver and connect differently. Building compassionate bridges across differences became natural when the conversation moved beneath the layers of identity and politics to a deeper humanity. I saw new possibilities for organizational leaders, systems, structures, and cultures—a transformation built around shifting the model from fear-based control to love-based liberation.

As you think about your journey, I ask you to consider the following:

- How do you define the soul-healing journey for yourself?
- What are you curious to explore as you embark on your own soul-healing journey?
- What would you like to let go of when you release from fear?
- What would you like to add to your life when you embrace love?
- What's holding you back from engaging in your soul-healing journey?

In the journey of healing and walking the soul-healing path, we deeply explore ourselves as men. We dive deep into our wounds, unmet needs, limiting beliefs, and shadows, uncovering the layers that have shaped our lives. Through awareness, compassion, and self-exploration, we begin to heal these parts of ourselves, integrating them into our being. We learn to forgive, cultivate self-compassion, and build supportive connections that guide us on our soul's calling.

Integrating spirituality, mindfulness, and embodiment practices, we align with our highest selves and discover a profound sense of purpose and connection. This transformative journey allows us to live authentically, liberated from the scripts and expectations that no longer serve us. We walk the soul-healing path, embracing love and experiencing the world with awe and wonderment, becoming catalysts for positive change in ourselves and the world around us.

CHAPTER 10

WALK THE SOUL-HEALING PATH

—

A shaman once told me the struggle for so many men center around the fact that they only have a few models of integrated fathers to look up to as they try to become more integrated men. Becoming integrated means reclaiming parts of ourselves we have rejected, denied, or suppressed. As we integrate the parts of ourselves we rejected, we unblock our wounds and become whole again. Forgiveness, compassion, and acceptance are critical ingredients for the soul-healing journey.

I am sharing a roadmap for soul healing that I walked, which I hope other men find helpful. I offer several different dimensions to the path at a high level. Without drilling down too deep, I will highlight my journey's most helpful healing steps. The collection of healing discussions below can offer new ways to think about healing. As you read each healing discussion, reflect on your life and whether the healing topic feels relevant to your journey and experience.

Healing the Spiritual Wounds

Healing the spiritual wounds is vital to the men's soul-healing journey by addressing disconnection from one's spiritual essence, loss of faith, and a sense of purposelessness. To begin healing, men must acknowledge their unique spiritual journey, exploring beliefs, values, and connections to the Divine. By recognizing areas of disconnection, they can initiate healing and restoration, seeking wholeness and alignment.

Reconnecting with one's spiritual essence involves exploring practices and traditions that resonate personally. Meditation, prayer, mindfulness, and nature-based spirituality can foster a deeper connection and inner peace. By engaging in these practices, men restore harmony and oneness with the natural world, promoting healing and growth.

Forgiveness and acceptance are essential in the healing journey, including self-forgiveness and forgiveness of others. Releasing resentments and judgments creates space for healing and invites spiritual growth. Cultivating compassion and nonjudgment allows the integration of past experiences, fostering peace and acceptance in the present moment.

Healing spiritual wounds is an ongoing process of self-reflection, inner work, and deepening spiritual understanding. It is a profoundly personal journey guided by inner wisdom and intuition. By addressing these wounds, men can experience transformation and find purpose, connection, and inner fulfillment on their soul-healing journey.

Cultivating Self-Compassion and Self-Forgiveness

Cultivating self-compassion and self-forgiveness are potent tools that enable men to embrace their humanity, let go of self-judgment, and nurture a kind and accepting relationship with themselves. Self-compassion involves extending the same warmth, care, and understanding toward oneself that one would offer to a loved one in times of difficulty or pain. It requires recognizing one's suffering, acknowledging it is a shared human experience, and responding with kindness and compassion.

Kristin Neff, a prominent researcher and expert in self-compassion, emphasizes the importance of self-forgiveness as a vital component of personal growth and healing. According to Neff, self-forgiveness involves recognizing our humanity and accepting that we are imperfect beings capable of making mistakes. It is about extending compassion, understanding, and kindness to ourselves, even in the face of our flaws and shortcomings. Neff believes that self-forgiveness is crucial for cultivating self-compassion, as it allows us to let go of self-criticism, self-judgment, and self-blame, which can hinder our personal growth and well-being (Neff 2015).

Individuals can develop a healthier and more supportive inner dialogue by cultivating self-compassion. This involves challenging the inner critic and replacing self-criticism with self-acceptance and self-nurturing messages. It means acknowledging one's imperfections, mistakes, and limitations without judgment or shame and offering oneself understanding and forgiveness.

Self-forgiveness is an integral part of self-compassion. It involves releasing oneself from past mistakes, regrets, and self-blame. Self-forgiveness acknowledges that everyone is fallible and capable of making errors, and it allows individuals to let go of resentment and negative emotions that keep them stuck in the past. Through self-forgiveness, individuals create space for healing, personal growth, and the opportunity to learn from past experiences without being defined by them.

Cultivating self-compassion and self-forgiveness is a lifelong practice that requires patience, commitment, and self-reflection. It involves developing mindfulness and self-awareness to recognize and challenge self-judgment and intentionally choosing self-compassion and forgiveness as guiding principles in daily life. Individuals can foster a more profound sense of self-worth, resilience, and inner peace by cultivating self-compassion and self-forgiveness, creating a foundation for personal growth, healing, and well-being.

Healing the Parental Wounds

In the introduction, I shared a little about the ways I healed my father wounds as I mended my relationship with my dad. However, there's more to the story. I couldn't attend my father's funeral because I was gay and his wife wouldn't allow it. I didn't hold any resentment and accepted her wishes.

While in seminary, I had a class assignment where I could create a funeral or memorial service and present it to my classmates. So, in this tradition, I designed a memorial service for my father. I could process any unresolved grief, anger, or sadness in this gesture. This allowed me to truly honor my father in all aspects of his humanity, which was a healing and cathartic moment that had most of the men in the class in tears as I closed out service with the song "Cats in the Cradle."

As I work with men around healing their father or mother wounds, I often suggest they take a symbolic gesture that acknowledges the wounds, offers space for forgiveness, and invites a deeper love into the relationship or memory of the parent. In my case, the memorial service was my symbolic gesture that was cathartic and healing. For others, I've suggested writing a letter, a poem, or a song to capture the feelings they are holding onto and seek to let go of, as well as the space for forgiveness and love. By healing my father wounds, it opened the door for me to begin working on my mother wounds.

My mother is still alive, and I've been deepening my relationship with her by the day. We are having conversations in ways we couldn't in the past. We can be honest about the past and hear each other differently in the present. Our unhealed wounds no longer distort how we hear and connect with each other.

Healing parental wounds is a transformative journey that empowers men to break free from the limitations and negative patterns shaped by their past experiences. The impact of our early relationships with parents or caregivers can influence our beliefs, emotions, and behaviors throughout our lives. By acknowledging the effects of parental wounds and delving into the depths of our emotions and memories, we can cultivate self-compassion and embark on a path of healing and self-discovery.

As part of the soul-healing journey, it is essential to recognize and accept the impact of parental wounds on our well-being. This requires courageously exploring the emotions, beliefs, and patterns our early experiences influenced.

Through self-reflection, therapy, and the support of nurturing communities, we can gain valuable insights and guidance on our healing journey.

Inner child work, therapy, journaling, and forgiveness are invaluable tools in healing parental wounds. By nurturing a compassionate and forgiving stance toward ourselves and our parents, we gradually release resentment and facilitate deep healing and transformation. Rebuilding a healthier relationship with our inner child by offering the love and support that may have been lacking in the past allows us to establish healthier patterns of relating, cultivate self-compassion, and forge more fulfilling connections with others.

Engaging in inner child work and re-parenting techniques enables us to connect with our wounded inner child, providing the care, love, and support they may have missed. By creating a new narrative of safety, love, and empowerment, we heal the wounds associated with childhood experiences. This involves acknowledging and processing the pain, anger, or sadness stemming from unmet needs, invalidation, or dysfunctional dynamics. Through compassionate self-reflection and forgiveness, we gain insight into how these wounds continue to impact our lives and relationships, transforming them into sources of strength, resilience, and deeper understanding.

Healing parental wounds is a personal and unique process that requires us to embrace vulnerability, acknowledge and express our emotions, and create a nurturing space for growth. We embark on a journey toward wholeness and well-being by fostering compassionate self-reflection, practicing forgiveness, and cultivating self-compassion. Through this transformative process, we reclaim our power, establish healthier patterns of relating, and gain a deeper understanding of ourselves and others. Ultimately, healing parental wounds empowers us to lead more fulfilling lives and foster stronger connections within ourselves and those around us.

Healing the Inner Child Wounds

I worked through my deepest inner child wounds during the shadow experience with Joe Laur and Sarah Schley. I would say two wounds stand out the most. First were the feelings of abandonment by not seeing my father for most of my childhood. However, the second and most significant was being molested by my babysitters at four years old. I shared how I healed my father wound around the abandonment earlier.

I worked through the second experience regarding my babysitters through shadow work. This was a psychodrama shadow experience in which I would interact with individuals and tap into the trauma from my past. The individuals playing my babysitters were volunteers from the local shadow work community. Each volunteer acted out a character so I could experience the past, tap into the feelings, and express what I needed to say that my four-year-old self couldn't. I could also rewrite the script of my narratives from that experience where those wounds no longer held me hostage. This was one of the most powerful experiences of my entire healing journey.

Healing the inner child is a fundamental aspect of a man's soul-healing journey, as it involves reconnecting with the wounded and neglected parts of oneself from childhood. The inner child represents our authentic self, filled with innocence, vulnerability, and natural joy. However, traumatic childhood experiences, emotional neglect, or unmet needs can cause the inner child to carry unresolved pain, fear, and limiting beliefs into adulthood.

The first step in healing the inner child is creating a safe and nurturing space for expression. This involves acknowledging and validating the emotions and experiences of the inner child without judgment or criticism. By offering compassion and understanding, men can develop a loving and accepting relationship with this wounded aspect of themselves.

The healing process also involves re-parenting the inner child. Men can provide the care, love, and support that may have been missing in their early years. This can be done through self-soothing techniques, inner-child visualization, and engaging in activities that bring joy and playfulness. By meeting the inner child's needs, men can restore a sense of wholeness, self-worth, and emotional well-being.

Healing the inner child requires inner work and self-reflection to identify and heal past wounds. It may involve seeking support from therapists or men's groups or engaging in inner-child healing practices. By embracing the inner child's experiences, releasing emotional burdens, and fostering self-compassion, men can embark on a transformative journey of self-discovery, emotional healing, and inner growth. Through this healing process, they can reclaim their authentic selves and cultivate a more profound sense of joy, creativity, and self-empowerment.

Healing Generational Trauma

Healing generational trauma is a profound journey for men to break free from the cycles of pain and dysfunction passed down through ancestral lines. It involves acknowledging the presence of generational trauma within one's own life and lineage and understanding the intergenerational patterns and behaviors that have influenced personal and familial dynamics. By exploring family history, creating safe spaces for emotional expression and release, engaging in intergenerational dialogue, and breaking harmful patterns, men can begin to heal.

The healing process requires cultivating self-compassion, forgiveness, and resilience. Men must extend compassion to themselves and their ancestors, recognizing trauma is not their fault but something they can work to heal. By developing healthier coping mechanisms, establishing boundaries, and cultivating positive relationships, men can break free from the chains of generational trauma.

While the journey is complex and challenging, it is possible with ongoing support from therapists, counselors, and trauma-informed practitioners. Through this transformative process, men reclaim their power, liberate themselves from the limitations of the past, and contribute to the healing of their families, communities, and collective consciousness. Healing generational trauma creates a new legacy of strength, healing, and emotional well-being for themselves and future generations, fostering resilience, growth, and a path toward a more vibrant and interconnected world.

Healing from Trauma, Shame, and Addiction

Healing shame, trauma, and addiction is a courageous journey that requires individuals to address deep emotional wounds and create a path toward personal growth and recovery. Shame, trauma, and addiction often intertwine, reinforcing the other in a complex cycle. Healing these interconnected challenges can involve self-reflection, self-compassion, therapy, and a commitment to personal transformation.

Shame is a profound and painful emotional response to a perceived failure or violation of societal or personal standards. This leads to unworthiness, self-judgment, and a desire to hide or withdraw. Shame that men experience can vary in its sources and manifestations, but it often relates to societal expectations and pressures surrounding masculinity.

Men may feel shame for not meeting traditional standards of strength, stoicism, dominance, or success. They might experience shame for expressing vulnerability and emotions or seeking help or support. The pressure to conform to narrow definitions of masculinity can create shame around perceived weaknesses or deviations from societal norms. Men may also experience shame related to body image, sexual performance, or their ability to fulfill societal roles as providers or protectors. Men's shame can be deeply ingrained and impact their mental health, self-esteem, and ability to form meaningful connections and seek support when needed.

Healing shame begins with acknowledging and understanding its roots and impact on one's life. It requires challenging and reframing negative self-beliefs, embracing vulnerability, and developing self-acceptance and self-compassion. Individuals can break free from shame's grip and foster a healthier self-image grounded in self-worth and self-love by cultivating self-compassion.

Trauma is a psychological and emotional response to an overwhelmingly distressing event or series of events that exceed an individual's capacity to cope and integrate the experience. It can result from many experiences, such as physical or sexual abuse, bullying, violence, accidents, natural disasters, or witnessing traumatic events. Trauma disrupts the sense of safety, trust, and stability, leaving individuals feeling overwhelmed, helpless, and disconnected. It can have long-lasting effects on various aspects of a person's life, including their emotions, cognition, relationships, and overall well-being. Trauma symptoms can include intrusive memories, flashbacks, nightmares, hypervigilance, emotional numbness, avoidance, and difficulties concentrating and sleeping.

Trauma healing often involves creating a safe space, addressing the impact of the traumatic experience, and supporting individuals in integrating and recovering from the effects. Addressing trauma is an essential component of the healing journey. It involves engaging in trauma-focused therapy, such as cognitive-behavioral therapy (CBT), Eye Movement Desensitization and Reprocessing (EMDR), or somatic experiencing. These therapeutic modalities help individuals process traumatic experiences, reframe their narratives, and develop healthy coping mechanisms to navigate life's challenges.

Addiction is a compulsive and chronic condition characterized by persistent engagement in substance use or behavior despite negative consequences, often accompanied by a loss of control and a strong craving for continued involvement. It involves the brain's reward systems, where the pursuit and consumption of a substance or engagement in a particular behavior become paramount, often leading to an inability to control or moderate behavior.

Historically, men have faced unique challenges and pressures that can contribute to their vulnerability to addiction. Traditional masculinity ideals that emphasize stoicism, self-reliance, and the suppression of emotions may discourage men from seeking help or expressing vulnerability, leading them to turn to substances or behaviors as a coping mechanism for stress, trauma, or masking emotional pain. Social factors, such as peer influence, societal norms around alcohol or drug use, and accessibility to substances, can further shape men's relationship with addiction.

Recovery from addiction requires a holistic approach that addresses the underlying emotional wounds and triggers. It typically involves engaging in therapy and support groups and building a solid support network. By developing healthy coping mechanisms, practicing self-care, and exploring alternative ways of finding fulfillment, individuals can break free from the cycle of addiction and build a life of recovery and well-being.

Healing shame, trauma, and addiction is not linear; it requires patience, commitment, and ongoing support. Through self-reflection, therapy, and embracing a compassionate mindset, individuals can reclaim their sense of self-worth, cultivate resilience, and embark on a transformative journey toward healing, personal growth, and a life filled with purpose and fulfillment.

Examining Men's Relationship to Gender

Examining men's relationship to gender involves exploring societal norms, expectations, and personal experiences. It profoundly reflects how gender influences their identities, beliefs, and behaviors. By examining their relationship to gender, men can foster self-awareness, challenge harmful stereotypes, and develop a more authentic and inclusive understanding of themselves and others.

To better understand the ways to examine gender, here are six distinctions that might be helpful:

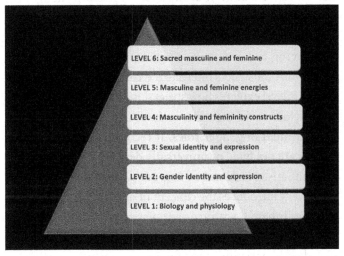

LEVEL 6: Sacred masculine and feminine

LEVEL 5: Masculine and feminine energies

LEVEL 4: Masculinity and femininity constructs

LEVEL 3: Sexual identity and expression

LEVEL 2: Gender identity and expression

LEVEL 1: Biology and physiology

(Image: Harvey 2023)

This model of examining gender provides a comprehensive framework for understanding the various dimensions and layers contributing to our understanding of gender.

At Level 1, gender is initially defined by our physiological and biological characteristics, such as our sex assigned at birth and our anatomical features. This serves as the foundation upon which other aspects of gender are built.

Level 2 delves into gender identity and expression, acknowledging that gender is not solely determined by biology. It recognizes that individuals may identify and express themselves in ways that align with or differ from societal expectations or traditional gender norms. This level highlights the importance of self-identification and embracing diverse expressions of gender.

Level 3 focuses on sexual identity and expression, recognizing that gender and sexuality are distinct but interconnected aspects of human experience. It acknowledges the diversity of sexual orientations and affirms the autonomy of individuals to define and express their own sexual identities.

Moving to Level 4, we encounter the masculinity and femininity constructs internalized through social conditioning. This level explores how societal messages, cultural norms, and various social institutions shape our understanding and embodiment of gender roles. It recognizes that these constructs are not fixed or universally defined but are subject to cultural, historical, and contextual variations.

Level 5 introduces the concept of masculine and feminine energies inherent within everyone regardless of gender identity. This level acknowledges that qualities traditionally associated with masculinity and femininity, such as assertiveness or nurturing, exist as universal human characteristics that individuals of any gender can express.

Level 6 invites us to explore the sacred masculine and feminine, transcending the binary constructs of gender and embracing a more spiritual and holistic perspective. It recognizes the inherent value and wisdom in masculine and feminine energies and encourages us to tap into them for personal growth, connection, and harmony.

Considering these six distinctions, we can deepen our understanding of gender and appreciate its multifaceted nature. This model highlights the complex interplay between biology, identity, expression, societal influences, and spiritual dimensions, ultimately fostering a more inclusive and nuanced understanding of gender in all its diversity.

As men, we had everything inside us when we were born: our masculine and feminine energies and qualities. As we grew older, many of us lost access to parts of ourselves, or as my dear friend Ken Mossman would say, we voted them off the island based on our conditioning or the messages we received from the world—our parents, friends, peers, faith, and media—that we internalized as our truth that informed our belief systems and worldview. For many men, we voted off our feminine attributes and have been left with our masculine energy, attributes, and qualities. This is not a question of right, wrong, good, or bad. However, what has been the cost, and what have you been missing by not accessing your feminine energy?

This exploration asks men to reflect on how societal expectations have shaped their understanding of masculinity and femininity. They can question the limitations and stereotypes associated with gender roles and critically analyze how these norms have influenced their perceptions and actions. By examining their internalized messages, men can liberate themselves from rigid gender constructs and embrace a more nuanced and fluid understanding of gender.

Brian Anderson, the author of *Fathering Together*, expounds upon this idea of liberating ourselves from rigid constructs by saying, "To fit the mold is at the base of everything. Let's tell men of all ages they don't have to fit the mold. We can break it. It'll hurt like hell, but it'll be much more life-giving without being broken."

Through self-reflection, open conversations, and engaging with diverse perspectives, men can expand their understanding of gender and embrace a more holistic approach to their identities. This journey invites men to develop greater empathy, cultivate healthy expressions of masculinity, and foster inclusive relationships. By examining their relationship to gender, men can actively contribute to creating a society that values and celebrates the full spectrum of gender identities and experiences.

Healing the Wounded Masculine, Sexism, and Internalized Homophobia

Healing the wounded masculine, addressing internal sexism, and confronting internalized homophobia are crucial aspects of a man's soul-healing journey. I often call these three areas of healing the "trifecta of constriction for men." The deep-seated wounds from this constriction can profoundly impact a man's sense of self, relationships, and overall well-being. By bringing awareness to these issues and actively engaging in healing, men can find liberation, authenticity, and wholeness.

Healing the wounded masculine involves acknowledging and addressing the societal conditioning and harmful narratives that have shaped traditional notions of masculinity. This includes exploring and challenging the beliefs and behaviors perpetuating hypermasculinity, such as rigid gender roles, emotional suppression, and the devaluation of femininity. By embracing a more expansive and inclusive understanding of masculinity, men can heal the wounds of societal expectations and create space for authentic self-expression, emotional depth, and healthy relationships.

Internal sexism refers to the internalization of societal sexism, which can lead to the devaluation and objectification of women and the suppression of feminine qualities within oneself. This internalized sexism can be harmful not only to women but also to men themselves, as it perpetuates unhealthy gender dynamics and limits personal growth. Healing internal sexism involves:

- Recognizing and challenging these deeply ingrained beliefs and behaviors.
- Fostering respect, equality, and collaboration between genders.
- Embracing the inherent worth and value of all individuals, regardless of gender.

Internalized homophobia is the internalization of negative societal attitudes and prejudices toward homosexuality or same-sex attraction. It can manifest as self-rejection, shame, and the denial of one's sexual orientation. Healing internalized homophobia requires self-acceptance, self-love, and embracing the diversity of sexual orientations. It involves confronting and challenging the societal messages that stigmatize and marginalize LGBTQ+ individuals, fostering empathy, and creating a safe and inclusive space for all sexual orientations.

Boysen Hodgson, communications director for the ManKind Project, shared that he believes homophobia keeps most men from doing the work—men's healing and transformation work. As he talked about his experience, the dominance hierarchy was so deeply embedded within him. In his role, he sees it in so many guys who come into the men's work.

He continued to share, "As men engage in the work and the feelings come to the surface, they begin to feel tenderness for other men. And they run the other way. It is so terrifying to feel tenderness for men. When men run up against that edge of discomfort, that is the edge to work. This is where you embrace your humanness. Most men would rather die than do that work."

As part of the soul-healing journey, men can explore these wounds by engaging in self-reflection, therapy, and supportive communities. Creating a safe and nonjudgmental space for men to examine their beliefs, experiences, and emotions is essential, releasing shame, guilt, and self-rejection. By developing emotional intelligence and vulnerability, men can confront and heal these wounds, cultivating a healthier and more authentic relationship with themselves and others.

Ultimately, healing the trifecta of constriction are transformative processes that allow men to break free from societal expectations, embrace their authentic selves, and cultivate healthy, balanced relationships. It is a journey of self-discovery, self-acceptance, and growth that fosters personal empowerment and contributes to the greater collective healing of gender-related wounds.

Healing through the Feminine

I often say that I did my men's work through the feminine while working at EF and during seminary. Then strengthened my masculine in Asheville and Washington, DC. Healing through the feminine is a transformative journey of rediscovering and embracing our feminine energy's innate power, wisdom, and nurturing qualities. It involves cultivating a deeper connection to our intuition, emotions, and authentic self-expression.

Creating a nurturing and compassionate space within ourselves is essential to embark on this path. This involves listening to our inner voice, acknowledging our emotions, and embracing self-care practices that restore balance. Through meditation, journaling, and creative expression, we tap into the depths of our feminine essence and access inner wisdom.

Yet embracing the feminine as part of the healing energy helps men strengthen their masculine. This is not about emasculating men but helping them integrate into their whole being with more skills, know-how, and agility in navigating and responding to the unexpected. This is how we become adaptive to an evolving world where we begin to respond rather than immediately react thoughtfully.

Through the healing journey of the feminine, we reclaim authenticity, strength, and resilience. We cultivate understanding, compassion, and purpose. Embracing the feminine within us allows us to navigate challenges with grace, intuition, and empathy, leading to wholeness, fulfillment, and embodying our true selves.

The wounded masculine and wounded feminine refer to the aspects within individuals that have been wounded or suppressed due to societal conditioning, gender stereotypes, and oppressive systems. The wounded masculine is often associated with traits such as aggression, dominance, and emotional detachment, while the wounded feminine is associated with qualities like submissiveness, passivity, manipulation, and self-sacrifice. Healing the wounded feminine involves reclaiming the power, intuition, and nurturing qualities of the feminine energy, fostering self-love, self-expression, and empowerment. Healing the wounded masculine involves:

- Transforming destructive behaviors and belief systems.
- Cultivating emotional intelligence.
- Embracing vulnerability.

- Healthy expressions of strength and assertiveness.

It is about finding balance and integration between these energies, embracing the healing qualities of both the feminine and masculine, and creating harmonious, authentic, and compassionate expressions of oneself.

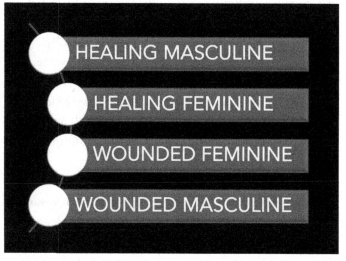

(Image: Harvey 2023)

Men's healing journeys often start in the wounded masculine, which holds the traditional conditions and teachings of manhood that can keep men locked in a place of constriction. As men walk their journey, they often move into the wounded feminine, where they begin to experience and feel into the feminine qualities while still operating in the shadow. Men start to heal in the healing feminine and ultimately strengthen through the healing masculine. This journey leads men to the integrated masculine and feminine.

Balancing the masculine and feminine is essential for experiencing wholeness and integration. It honors both energies' unique strengths and qualities and fosters a more holistic expression of self. By embracing assertiveness, compassion, strength, and nurturing, we tap into a broader range of potentials, creating authentic relationships and contributing to societal transformation.

Balancing the Masculine and Feminine Energies

Finding a balance between masculine and feminine energies is integral to men's soul-healing journey. Society often emphasizes rigid gender roles and expectations that can limit men's self-expression and emotional well-being. However, by embracing and integrating masculine and feminine qualities, men can cultivate a deeper sense of wholeness, authenticity, and inner harmony. Here are four areas where men can find a greater balance to bring them into their integrated selves.

- **Balancing vulnerability and authenticity.** Society often places emphasis on masculine traits such as strength, assertiveness, and independence, which can discourage vulnerability and authenticity. However, by embracing their feminine qualities, men can tap into their vulnerability, openness, and willingness to be seen authentically. This allows for deeper connections and intimacy in relationships, as vulnerability creates space for trust, understanding, and emotional support.

- **Balancing action and stillness.** The masculine energy is often associated with action, achievement, and productivity, while the feminine embodies receptivity, intuition, and reflection. Men are encouraged to find a harmonious balance between taking purposeful action and allowing themselves moments of stillness and introspection. This balance nurtures self-care, self-reflection, and a deeper connection with inner wisdom, leading to a more grounded and fulfilling existence.

- **Balancing individuality and interconnectedness.** The masculine energy often celebrates individuality, autonomy, and self-reliance, while the feminine energy emphasizes the interconnectedness of all beings. Men can foster balance by valuing their unique strengths and identities while recognizing the importance of collaboration, empathy, and compassion in building meaningful relationships and creating a sense of community. This integration supports men in embracing their authentic selves while fostering deeper connections with others.

- **Balancing strength and sensitivity.** The masculine energy traditionally emphasizes physical strength, resilience, and assertiveness, while the feminine embodies emotional sensitivity, nurturing, and intuition. Men can benefit from cultivating both qualities within themselves, recognizing that strength does not negate sensitivity and that sensitivity can coexist with strength. This integration allows men to show up authentically, express their emotions, and engage in nurturing relationships, leading to greater emotional well-being and connection with others.

As men embrace balancing the masculine and feminine energies within themselves, they lay the foundation for the next phase of their soul-healing journey—integrating the sacred masculine and feminine. This integration goes beyond mere balance and seeks to unite and harmonize these energies into a sacred dance within the core of their being. It is a transformative process that invites men to explore the depths of their true nature, embodying the qualities of strength, compassion, assertiveness, receptivity, intuition, and action in a harmonious union.

Integrating the Sacred Feminine and Sacred Masculine

As men integrate the sacred masculine and feminine, they tap into their authentic power, wisdom, and love, allowing them to lead fulfilling lives, nurture healthy relationships, and contribute to the collective healing of humanity. This integration invites men to embrace and harmonize the qualities and energies traditionally associated with masculinity and femininity.

The sacred masculine represents strength, assertiveness, and logic, while the sacred feminine embodies compassion, intuition, and nurturing. Integrating these aspects allows men to access a more complete and authentic expression of themselves. It is not about favoring one over the other or seeking dominance but rather about embracing the full spectrum of human experience and potential.

This integration teaches men to embody the sacred masculine by cultivating self-awareness, setting healthy boundaries, and engaging in self-reflection. We embrace our strengths and assertiveness, using them to serve our purpose and the greater good. At the same time, we honor the sacred feminine by nurturing our intuition, cultivating compassion and empathy, and creating space for vulnerability and emotional connection.

Integrating the sacred masculine and sacred feminine creates a foundation for deeper and more fulfilling relationships. We learn to communicate authentically, listen with empathy, and hold space for others. We embrace collaboration and cooperation, valuing diverse perspectives and contributions. This integration allows for a more harmonious and balanced approach to relating with others, fostering connection, understanding, and mutual growth.

Matthew Fox, the spiritual theologian and author of *The Hidden Spirituality of Men: Ten Metaphors to Awaken the Sacred Masculine*, shares his perspective on integrating the sacred masculine and feminine. He views sacred masculinity as an essential aspect of spirituality overlooked or undervalued in traditional religious and societal frameworks. He emphasizes the need to reclaim and embrace the positive qualities associated with masculinity in a balanced and holistic manner (Fox 2008).

According to Fox, sacred masculinity embodies strength, courage, leadership, protection, and action. However, he also highlights the importance of integrating these qualities with compassion, empathy, sensitivity, and respect for others. He promotes a vision of masculinity that honors the assertive and nurturing aspects of the human experience, fostering a sense of interconnectedness and harmony.

Fox encourages men to embark on a spiritual journey that involves healing past wounds, examining cultural conditioning, and rediscovering their authentic selves. He believes that through this process, men can access their innate spirituality and contribute positively to the world.

Integrating the sacred masculine and sacred feminine is a profound journey of self-discovery and self-realization. It invites men to transcend societal conditioning and embrace the fullness of their being. By harmonizing these energies within themselves, they become more activated as change agents, fostering a more compassionate, balanced, and interconnected world.

As you think about your journey, I ask you to consider the following:

- What resonated for you most when reading through this chapter?
- What challenged you most when reading through this chapter?
- What healing discussions feel most relevant for you as you think about your journey?
- Which of these discussions are you curious to learn more about and explore further?
- What healing actions are you interested in taking next?

Walking the soul-healing path requires courage, self-reflection, and a willingness to confront deep emotional wounds. By embracing emotional intelligence, cultivating vulnerability and authenticity, balancing action and stillness, honoring individuality and interconnectedness, and integrating strength and sensitivity, men can embark on a path of healing and growth. Through this inner work, men can heal relationship wounds, liberate themselves from societal expectations, and create healthier and more fulfilling connections with themselves and others.

By integrating the sacred masculine and feminine energies, men can tap into their authentic power, wisdom, and love, paving the way for a more harmonious and interconnected world. The journey of healing relationship wounds is an ongoing process. However, with each step taken, men move closer to experiencing greater wholeness, compassion, and the ability to create transformative change in their lives and the lives of those around them.

CHAPTER 11

EXPAND YOUR CAPACITY TO LOVE

———

I remember having a frank conversation with my doctor while living in New York City. During my visit, I asked him how he defined healthy sexuality based on his forty years as a primary care physician. He took my question seriously and replied:

> "Sean, I've seen it all over the years. When I think about it, I believe it all comes down to intimacy. You have to ask yourself, when you are having sex, are you running toward intimacy or running away from it?"

I sat with his answer for days and was struck by the profound simplicity of his response. It spurred my thinking about this topic centered around love, sex, and intimacy. We live in a time when it's easy to find faux intimacy with the countless dating and hookup apps, open relationships, the barrage of social media posts and reels, and limited time in people's schedules to create meaningful connections.

In my work in the personal transformation space, the work around love, intimacy, and relationships is usually the final frontier for the healing journey. Relationships show us who we are as we see ourselves through someone else's eyes. Intimacy often shows us our wounds and where our fears exist on a deeper level. This is the space where we quickly realize what triggers or activates us and the unresolved issues that continue to follow us. We will explore new ways to expand our capacity to love as men starting with healing our relationship wounds.

Healing Relationship Wounds

Living in New York City, I didn't think much about dating or relationships. After my breakup from my seven-year relationship, I enjoyed casual dating and hooking up with no attachments. At that point in my life, finding a relationship in Manhattan felt almost as impossible as having the down payment for a two-million-dollar apartment in Brooklyn. It took me a good year to get over my seven-year relationship. Today, my ex and I are like brothers. While we do not see or talk with each other frequently, we are there for each other if we need something.

After seminary, I felt ready to start dating again. Yes, as an interfaith minister, I can date and get married. After leaving New York City, I tried dating in Asheville and Washington, DC. My dating attempts in Asheville were a series of crash-and-burn experiences. I experienced a lot of ghosting and heard, "You want more than I can give," or "You're too intense," a few too many times.

After I moved to Washington, my dating experiences were even worse. The first guy I went out with told me on the first date that he'd been arrested for beating up his last boyfriend, who was a monk. I also tried to rekindle a spark back in Asheville, which was a complete disaster. On my drive back to Washington at two in the morning, I had time to reflect on my dating life.

During that drive, an old tape (limiting belief) I had lived with my entire life registered as "nobody would ever want me." That phrase kept playing in my head over and over throughout that drive home. When I could finally hear it, I realized this internal belief was at the core of my relationship challenges, and I needed to look deeper. I was ready to start looking at my relationship wounds and the root of my challenges to find and experience love.

Healing relationship wounds is vital to men's healing journeys, as past experiences can shape their beliefs, behaviors, and emotional well-being in relationships. To support men in healing these wounds, it is essential to create safe and nurturing spaces where they can explore and process their experiences and emotions. Providing therapy, support groups, or men's circles allows men to share their stories, gain insights from others, and receive validation and empathy.

Self-reflection involves examining patterns, triggers, and beliefs contributing to relationship challenges. By developing self-awareness and taking responsibility for their actions and healing, men can break free from destructive cycles and establish healthier relationship patterns.

Supportive relationships play a significant role in helping men heal their relationship wounds. Surrounding themselves with compassionate, understanding individuals who can provide emotional support and guidance is invaluable. Open and honest conversations with trusted friends, partners, or mentors allow men to explore their wounds, gain new perspectives, and receive feedback. Building a support network that encourages vulnerability and growth fosters a sense of belonging and facilitates healing in relationships.

By creating nurturing spaces, cultivating self-compassion and self-reflection, and fostering supportive relationships, we can empower men to heal their relationship wounds. Through this process, men can develop healthier patterns, establish deeper connections, and experience greater emotional well-being in their relationships. Healing relationship wounds is a transformative process that allows men to cultivate fulfilling and authentic connections with themselves and others.

Understanding Attachment Styles

As I said earlier, one of my core limiting beliefs discovered in this process is that nobody would ever want me. This led to many failed attempts at dating and relationships. As I started to dig into the causes of my relationship challenges, I realized I'd either come off too strong or wanted to jump in quickly to get the validation I sought. If someone came along who was well-adjusted and already engaged in their healing work, I would typically find them boring and move on quickly. I can attribute some of this to my anxious attachment style.

Attachment styles play a crucial role in shaping our patterns of relating and forming intimate connections. By exploring and understanding their attachment styles, men can gain valuable insights into their relational dynamics.

Attachment theory suggests our early experiences with caregivers shape our attachment styles, influencing how we approach and experience relationships throughout our lives. The three main attachment styles are secure, anxious, and avoidant (Levine and Heller 2012).

- **Secure Attachment Style**
  Men with a secure attachment style are comfortable with intimacy and autonomy. They have a favorable view of themselves and others and can effectively communicate their needs and emotions. They can establish healthy boundaries, seek support when needed, and navigate relationship challenges with resilience and trust.

- **Anxious Attachment Style**
  Men with an anxious attachment style seek high levels of closeness and worry about their partner's availability and commitment. They often experience fear of abandonment and have a strong desire for reassurance and validation. They may exhibit clingy behavior, become overly preoccupied with their relationships, and tend to interpret ambiguous situations negatively.

- **Avoidant Attachment Style**
  Men with an avoidant attachment style value independence and may feel uncomfortable with too much intimacy or dependency. They prioritize self-reliance and may struggle with emotional vulnerability. They tend to downplay the importance of relationships, suppress their emotions, and have difficulty expressing their needs or seeking support.

For men on their soul-healing journey, it is essential to delve into attachment styles and understand how they impact their relationships. Recognizing and understanding one's attachment style can help shed light on patterns of behavior, emotional responses, and challenges in forming and maintaining intimate connections. By gaining insight into their attachment style, men can identify and address unhealthy patterns or insecurities that may hinder their ability to create deep and fulfilling relationships.

Exploring attachment styles also allows men to cultivate self-compassion and healing. It allows them to recognize their attachment style is not a fixed trait but a product of their upbringing and past experiences. Understanding that attachment styles can be modified and healed empowers men to embark on a journey of self-reflection, personal growth, and healing. By developing secure attachment patterns, men can foster healthier, more fulfilling relationships grounded in trust, emotional availability, and authentic connection.

By integrating an understanding of attachment styles into their soul-healing journey, men can navigate relationships with greater self-awareness and empathy. This exploration invites men to reflect on their attachment needs, learn practical communication skills, and develop the capacity for emotional intimacy. By embracing vulnerability and cultivating specific attachment patterns, men can create and sustain deeply fulfilling relationships that support their growth and well-being.

Untethering Love, Sex, and Intimacy

This was one of the most essential steps in my journey to expand my capacity to love. I had to distinguish between love, sex, and intimacy. While seeking deeper intimacy and connection, I settled for crumbs with cheap and meaningless sex. It might have been because I was tired of trying, maybe because I had such low self-worth, or maybe I was too afraid to be vulnerable, and the fear of rejection was so great. Looking back, it was a combination of all three. A friend likened hookups to eating a bag of potato chips: they have no nutritional value, and you cannot eat just one.

I was trying to fill the void of my inability to love myself or see my worth through a series of hookups. I was deluding myself by thinking that I could find love when I could not love myself. As I said at the beginning of this book, I needed a roadmap because I had no clue how to love myself when I started this journey. This is where I focused a lot of my attention on my healing; it was the final frontier work for me on this journey.

This untethering work is crucial in a man's journey to have healthy and loving relationships. Untethering begins with self-reflection and self-discovery, inviting individuals to explore their needs, desires, and beliefs about sex, love, and intimacy. It requires questioning and shedding preconceived notions that may limit or restrict the authentic expression of these aspects of human connection.

When talking about untethering love, sex, and intimacy with men, I often say that for most men:

"It's the intimacy we yearn for,
the love we misunderstand,
and the sex we settle for."

By untethering sex, love, and intimacy, men can cultivate healthier and more fulfilling relationships. It enables them to communicate their needs and boundaries more effectively, fostering mutual understanding and consent. Untethering also allows for greater exploration and self-discovery of one's deepest desires, leading to a more authentic expression of a man's truth in his relationship with himself and others.

Through untethering, men can develop a more comprehensive and nuanced understanding of themselves and their relationships. It empowers them to navigate these aspects of human connection with authenticity, respect, and open-mindedness, ultimately fostering more satisfying and harmonious relationships with others.

Men can untether by challenging the notion that love and intimacy must be solely linked to sexual activity. By recognizing love and intimacy can exist in various forms, such as emotional connection, deep conversations, shared experiences, and acts of kindness, men can broaden their understanding of intimacy beyond purely sexual interactions. This shift allows for more meaningful and fulfilling connections based on emotional depth, vulnerability, and mutual respect.

Men can liberate themselves from the pressure to perform or conform to rigid ideals of masculinity that prioritize sexual conquest or objectification. This entails embracing and expressing their authentic desires, preferences, and boundaries while actively seeking enthusiastic consent and ensuring equal participation and pleasure for all involved. By untethering these aspects, men can foster healthier relationships, promote emotional well-being, and cultivate a more compassionate and egalitarian approach to love, sex, and intimacy.

Unblocking Intimacy to Access Love

If intimacy is what men most yearn for but rarely talk about, what is it, and why must it be unblocked?

Intimacy is a deeply connected and authentic emotional, physical, or spiritual closeness between individuals. It goes beyond surface interactions and involves profound trust, vulnerability, and mutual understanding. Intimacy can exist within various relationships, including romantic partnerships, sexual relationships, among family members, or friendships.

Jim Young, a friend, colleague, and men's coach says expansive intimacy (also the name of his book) becomes possible when we agree to willingly reveal our closely held beliefs, thoughts, feelings, needs, desires, ideas, and experiences to another person, with a spirit of openness and reciprocity, thereby creating a stronger, more fulfilled relationship (Young 2022).

The journey to unblock intimacy that has often been constricted due to conditioning and shaped by life experience enables men to cultivate deeper connections and access the transformative power of love. Intimacy involves being vulnerable, emotionally present, and authentically connected with others. However, past experiences, traumas, and societal conditioning can create barriers that hinder the expression of intimacy and prevent individuals from fully experiencing love.

To unblock intimacy, men must first engage in self-reflection and self-awareness. This involves exploring and understanding their fears, insecurities, and past experiences that may have shaped their approach to intimacy. By gaining insight into these barriers, men can start dismantling them and fostering a greater sense of self-acceptance and self-love.

Healing and releasing past wounds is a crucial step in unblocking intimacy. This may involve therapy, self-help practices, or seeking support from trusted individuals. By addressing past traumas, negative beliefs, and emotional blocks, men can create space for intimacy to flourish and access a deeper sense of connection and love.

Building healthy communication skills and practicing vulnerability is essential in unblocking intimacy. This includes expressing emotions authentically, actively listening, and creating a safe space for open and honest conversations. By embracing vulnerability, men allow themselves to be seen and known, creating the potential for deeper connections and the experience of profound love.

Through unblocking intimacy, individuals can access love in its fullest expression. By cultivating self-awareness, healing past wounds, and embracing vulnerability, men can create the conditions for love to flow freely. Unblocking intimacy allows men to connect more deeply with themselves and others, fostering authentic and fulfilling relationships rooted in love, understanding, and emotional connection.

Expanding Men's Capacity to Love

The wounding that many men experience prevents them from fully experiencing, embodying, and expressing love. The ego protects us from being vulnerable but also prevents us from tapping into the transforming power of love. This exploration is about helping men tap into the type of love that allows for genuine authenticity, deep connection, meaningful purpose, and compassion-centered, soul-inspired leadership.

We, as men, need to unpack the wounding and conditioning that keeps us from experiencing and tapping into love.

bell hooks, the well-known author of the bestselling book *A Will to Change: Men, Masculinity, and Love,* argues that patriarchy and traditional notions of masculinity often limit men's access to love. She highlights how societal expectations of masculinity enforce a stoic and emotionally closed-off demeanor, discouraging men from expressing vulnerability and seeking emotional support. This limited expression of emotions and affection can inhibit men's ability to fully experience and access love in their relationships (hooks 2004).

Hooks emphasizes the importance of dismantling patriarchal norms and encouraging a culture of emotional openness and vulnerability for men. She advocates for creating spaces where men can engage in emotional expression, introspection, and self-reflection without fear of judgment or retribution. By challenging rigid gender roles and fostering healthy emotional connections, men can cultivate deeper and more fulfilling experiences of love and intimacy.

That is what this journey and this book are all about. Helping men learn to love the truth of who they are once they discover and reclaim who they are. When I say love yourself, I mean love all parts of yourself that you do not always love, including those you do not let others see and those you don't want to see for yourself. This may be where you feel shame or regret in ways that activate uncontrollable fear or rage. Much of our hidden parts or those behind protective layers come from a place of fear. Often our greatest fear as men is having those parts of ourselves seen by ourselves or others.

The antidote to fear is leaning into the transforming power of love, which is at the root of compassion. As men, we can operate from a place of love or fear. By tapping into love, we permit ourselves to be courageous to look deep within, to be in an inquiry, and to discover the truth of who we are without fear, shame, or regret. This opens the door to more authentically connecting with ourselves and others from a place of deeper intimacy.

As you think about your journey, I ask you to consider the following:

- How would you describe your healing or wounding regarding love and relationships?
- What are your reactions to untethering love, sex, and intimacy?
- What holds you back from giving and receiving unconditional love?
- How do you show unconditional love to yourself?
- What will help you love more fully, deeply, and unconditionally?

The journey to expanding our capacity to love is profound and transformative. It requires us to heal relationship wounds, understand our attachment styles, untether love, sex, and intimacy, and unblock intimacy to access the transformative power of love. Through this journey, we can break free from societal conditioning, dismantle limiting beliefs, and cultivate authentic connections with ourselves and others. We open ourselves to the immense possibilities of deep, fulfilling, and loving relationships by embracing vulnerability, self-reflection, and self-compassion. This work is not easy, but it is necessary for personal growth and healing while creating a more compassionate and connected world.

Until we can access and embrace the transforming power of love, as men, we often remain stuck in our wounding, steeped in fear, resentment, and shame. Love is the life force that transforms us into who we are called to be in the world. At the root of warrior compassion is love. This is the antidote to the trauma wounds from a place of disconnection, isolation, loneliness, and detachment from one's emotions. Yet many men are shut off from love. Men often misunderstand love. It is the thing that eludes most men. The healing power of warrior compassion is designed to open our hearts to ourselves so we can face any challenge or obstacle with love, compassion, and curiosity.

PART V

UNLEASHING THE HEALING POWER

———

A Healing Warrior's Prayer
for Transformation

—SEAN HARVEY, INTERFAITH AND
INTERSPIRITUAL MINISTER

Divine Spirit, we ask that you bless this healing path that
    men are being called to walk.
Illuminate a new way forward and carry them through the
    twists and turns of the journey.
Provide them the ability to listen in the silence and the
    courage to walk into the unknown.
Empower men to relax their ego and walk from a place of
    curiosity and wonderment.

Reveal to men the sacred compass that connects them to
    their inner knowing.
Give them the strength to embrace whatever emerges on
    the path with love, light, and wisdom.
Bring these men to new discoveries through their own
    inquiry, truth, and light.
Offer them hope in their darkest hours and a bright light
    to a new liberation of their being.

Ignite a creative spark through play and imagination to see
    the world in new ways.
Impart your message of love through each interaction
    among their fellow travelers.

Invite authentic connection that flows from being to being
and soul to soul.
Transform each man's perspective from fear-based control
to love-based liberation.

Deepen each man's level of consciousness, compassion,
and connection radiating from within.
Create new possibilities for healing and transformation
from this place of conscious awareness.
Activate each man in his capacity to build bridges and
transform systems from a place of love.
May men be restored, transformed, and inspired to
co-create a compassionate world for all.

CHAPTER 12

EMERGE AS A HEALING WARRIOR

———

To better understand the journey of a healing warrior, let's begin by defining the concept. A healing warrior can be described as a man who combines strength, resilience, and courage with a deep commitment to personal growth, healing, and the well-being of oneself and others.

Healing Warrior Qualities and Characteristics

Unlike the wounded warrior, the healing warrior recognizes true strength is not just physical but also encompasses emotional, mental, and spiritual aspects. They understand healing is a transformative journey that requires deep inner work and compassion toward oneself and others.

They embody a unique approach to life, walking from a place of curiosity and wonderment rather than a mindset of all-knowing. They release the ego's need to be right or righteous, allowing themselves to be open to new possibilities.

The healing warrior creates space for growth, learning, and a deeper understanding by embracing a state of not knowing. They walk the path of self-discovery and growth, relinquishing the need to hold onto rigid beliefs. By relaxing the ego and letting go of preconceived notions, the healing warrior opens themselves to the vastness of the unknown, allowing new perspectives and insights to emerge.

On their journey, they seek to discover and experience the power of community and work through their obstacles and barriers to deeper connection. They understand that the dark nights of the soul, those moments of profound challenge and introspection, are critical to the healing journey. However, they also recognize healing and growth come from the support, love, and understanding of others. Within the context of a community, the wounded warrior begins to experience joy, laughter, and peace. As a dear friend, mentor, and father figure, David Berry used to tell me regularly, "While we have been harmed in relationships, we will be healed in relationships."

Fearlessly embracing life's obstacles that offer valuable lessons and opportunities for personal growth. Rather than avoiding or suppressing their wounds, they bravely face them head on. With a sense of curiosity and an open heart, a man on his healing journey delves into the depths of his being, seeking to uncover the core wounding that keeps him trapped in fear, resentment, and shame. This process of self-inquiry and exploration allows him to gain a deeper understanding of himself and the patterns that hold him back, paving the way for healing and liberation.

One of the essential steps on the journey is removing the mask of the constructed identity. Often created for self-protection, this mask no longer serves their growth and authenticity. With courage and vulnerability, the healing warrior peels away the layers of pretense and polish, allowing their true essence to shine through. By embracing their authentic self, they become free from societal expectations and external judgments and forge a path that is true to their values, passions, and desires.

Deep listening becomes a transformative practice. Healing men learn to listen to the external world and the wisdom that resides within. Each man gains profound guidance and insight by tapping into their embodied wisdom and inner knowing. This internal listening allows them to make aligned decisions, navigate challenges with clarity and grace, and connect with their deepest desires and purpose.

With unwavering courage, each man's gaze turns inward, exploring their unmet needs and confronting limiting beliefs that have held them back. They embark on a journey of self-discovery, examining the shadow aspects of themselves that have been rejected, suppressed, or hidden away. This courageous exploration leads to a profound reclamation and integration of these disowned parts, fostering self-acceptance, compassion, and wholeness. By embracing their shadows, wounded men free themselves from shame and step into a more authentic and empowered version of themselves.

Father Richard Rohr is an American Franciscan Priest and well-regarded writer and scholar on spirituality. He shares that within each of us lie the true and false selves. The true self, he says, is what religion often calls the soul—your eternal essence. The false self is the persona you create for yourself. Father Richard believes your goal in life is to find and manifest your true self.

He speaks about his soul-healing work with men in this way: "In our work with men, we have found that in many men, this inability or refusal to feel their deep sadness takes the form of aimless anger. The only way to get to the bottom of their anger is to face the ocean of sadness underneath it. Men are not free to cry, so they just transmute their tears into anger, and sometimes it pools up in their soul in the form of real depression. Men are actually encouraged to deny their shadow self in any competitive society, so we all end up with a lot of sad and angry old men. Men are capable of so much more, if they will only do some shadowboxing" (Rohr 2011).

The healing warrior recognizes the importance of breaking down the walls within himself and in his relationships. He lives into his truth and develops healthy boundaries that honor his needs and values. Healing men create a space of safety and respect by setting clear boundaries, allowing authentic connections to flourish. He communicates openly and honestly, fostering deep, meaningful relationships built on trust, vulnerability, and mutual growth.

Central to the journey is the discovery and love of their true essence. The healing warrior embarks on a profound exploration of self, seeking to understand his inherent gifts, strengths, and unique qualities. By peeling back the layers of conditioning and societal expectations, he uncovers the truth of who he is at his core. This process of self-discovery allows him to embrace his authentic self with love and acceptance, nurturing a deeper sense of self-worth and self-love.

The Mission of the Healing Warrior

The journey extends beyond healing warriors and encompasses love and compassion for all living beings and the planet. They recognize the interconnectedness of all life and expand their loving presence and care to the world around them. With deep empathy and compassion, these men become stewards of the Earth, nurturing and protecting the natural world and all its inhabitants.

According to Robert Augustus Masters, when men engage in their healing process and address their wounds, traumas, and conditioning, they experience personal transformation and become agents of change in their communities and society. He suggests that as men heal and embody authentic masculinity, they bring forth qualities such as compassion, empathy, emotional intelligence, and vulnerability. These qualities challenge the prevailing norms of masculinity that perpetuate harm and allow men to contribute to a more compassionate, just, and harmonious world (Masters 2018).

Masters emphasizes the importance of men reclaiming their emotional range and cultivating a deeper understanding of their own needs and the needs of others. By doing so, men can build healthier relationships, foster human connections, and create spaces for dialogue and healing. He suggests that through their transformative presence, healed men can inspire others to embark on their healing journeys, creating a ripple effect extending beyond individual relationships and into families, communities, and society.

Leading from a place of service, purpose, and deeper consciousness, the healing warrior becomes a beacon of light and inspiration as he activates his inner change agent. He embraces his power from within, challenging the status quo and fearlessly speaking truth to power. He invites others to join him in exploring ways to transform systems and structures through a lens of compassion and deeper humanity. His approach is rooted in love-based empowerment and liberation, advocating for a world that uplifts and benefits everyone rather than a select few.

By cultivating his own healing and growth, he becomes a catalyst for change. He inspires others to embark on their healing journeys by sharing his authenticity, compassion, and wisdom. The embodiment and energetic resonance of the healing warrior's presence and energy invites transformation and healing. These healing men foster a collective awakening and an emergence of a more compassionate, just, and harmonious world.

The men walking this path of self-discovery, growth, and transformation embody the qualities of curiosity, vulnerability, courage, and love. Each step deepens his understanding of himself and his connection to the world. The journey of the healing warrior is a profound exploration of the human spirit, a quest for personal liberation and collective healing, and an unwavering commitment to love, service, and the empowerment of all.

As you think about your journey, I ask you to consider the following:

- What's stirring in you as you read this chapter?
- What does it mean to you to become a healing warrior?
- What qualities do you possess as a healing warrior?
- What do you understand about your mission at this stage in your journey?
- What impact do you want to make in the world?
- How do you want to further develop as a healing warrior?

The journey of the healing warrior is a profound call to men, inviting them to step into their authentic selves with courage, vulnerability, and love. It is a path of self-discovery, healing, and growth that transcends societal expectations and embraces the true essence of who they are. By dismantling the constructs of masculinity, exploring their wounds, embracing their shadows, and cultivating deep self-love and compassion, men can emerge as powerful agents of change and transformation.

The healing warrior embodies the qualities of empathy, resilience, and a commitment to the well-being of themselves and others. Their actions and presence inspire a collective awakening and the creation of a more compassionate and just world. The healing path is an invitation to embrace one's true essence, walk with curiosity and wonder, and bring healing and love to every step of the journey.

CHAPTER 13

DISCOVER YOUR SOUL'S MISSION

———

Most of what I've shared throughout this book reflects my journey to discover and carry out my soul's mission. The soul's mission is the sacred contract each individual carries within them, intricately woven into the fabric of their spiritual journey. It is a profound calling from the depths of the soul, guided by higher forces and divine wisdom.

The soul's mission involves exploring and realizing one's divine purpose, seeking to align with the higher self, and contributing to the evolution of consciousness, love, compassion, and truth in all aspects of existence. It is a profound spiritual quest that unfolds through self-discovery, awakening, and the integration of divine guidance, ultimately expanding one's soul and collective consciousness.

This path requires us to listen to the whispers of our hearts, embrace vulnerability, and align with our values and higher principles. As we connect with the divine and cultivate self-awareness, we unearth our inherent gifts and follow our genius, allowing our authentic essence to guide us. Along this journey, we must be open to experimentation, pay attention to the doors that open effortlessly, and embrace the discomfort of vulnerability and taking risks.

This quest is not linear or logical; it is a sacred and transformative process that invites us to reflect on our stories, find patterns, and learn from our challenges. Through deep reflection, we understand the brilliance of the universe's design, shaping us for our purpose and mission in life. Embracing the joy and playfulness of the journey, we practice patience and embrace the expansiveness of our mission. As we discover our soul's calling, we tap into a profound sense of fulfillment, knowing that our unique contributions can help transform the world. The journey of discovering our soul's mission is a lifelong endeavor, a testament to our growth, and an invitation to live a purposeful and meaningful life.

Embarking on the journey of discovering your soul's mission is an extraordinary quest that invites you to explore the depths of your being, unearth your unique gifts, and align with a greater purpose. It is a transformative path beyond mere career choices or external achievements, delving into the essence of who you are and why you are here. Discovering your soul's mission is about connecting with the core of your being, listening to the whispers of your heart, and embracing the profound impact you can make in the world. It invites you to live a purposeful, meaningful life that aligns with your authentic self.

By engaging in our inner work, men will most likely feel an inherent call to serve. However, by going on the journey, it's safe to say their worldview has evolved. They see the suffering in the world differently and become more inclined to reduce it. This is usually reflected in their own experience and breakthroughs. Engaging in our purpose and mission work is about discovering the truth of who we are, why we came into being in this lifetime, what we are called to do, and the mission we are destined to carry out in this life.

In a world often driven by external expectations, societal pressures, and the pursuit of material success, the search for one's soul mission becomes an act of reclaiming personal sovereignty and reconnecting with the deepest aspects of our humanity. It is an invitation to move beyond the surface-level desires and societal definitions of success and dive into the realm of purpose intricately woven into our existence's fabric. Discovering your soul's mission is an invitation to peel back the layers of conditioning, transcend limited beliefs, and rediscover the unique purpose that awaits you.

Discovering your soul's mission requires deep listening, reflection, creativity, experimentation, and curiosity. In some ways, you must suspend what feels literal and logical, which makes sense based on the career decisions you've made throughout your life. Your true calling, purpose, and mission work will stem from the wisdom and truth of your soul.

Gary Zukav, in his book *The Seat of the Soul*, explores the concept of discovering and aligning with one's soul purpose. He suggests everyone contributes uniquely to the world, and connecting with that purpose is essential for personal fulfillment and spiritual growth (Zukav 1989).

According to Zukav, discovering one's soul purpose involves moving beyond the external trappings of success, such as wealth or status, and delving into the depths of one's inner being. He emphasizes the importance of introspection, self-reflection, and self-awareness as tools for uncovering one's true calling. Zukav proposes that the soul's purpose is intricately connected to love and compassion. He suggests that when individuals align with their soul's purpose, they tap into a deep reservoir of love and contribute to the well-being of others. Individuals can fulfill their purpose and impact the world meaningfully by cultivating empathy, kindness, and service.

Listen to Your Inner Wisdom

As you explore your soul's mission, the first step is to cultivate a state of inner stillness and listen to the wisdom that resides within you. Create moments of quiet in your life when you can detach from external distractions and turn your attention to the whispers of your inner voice. In these precious moments, you can tap into your inner wisdom, that sacred compass that guides you toward your true purpose.

Instead of relying on external sources, turn your gaze inward and seek guidance from your own inner knowing. Engage in practices such as meditation, reflection, and introspection to connect with the depths of your being. By quieting the mind's chatter and opening your heart, you create space for intuitive whispers to emerge. Trust in the insights, feelings, and sensations that arise, for they are the language of your inner wisdom, providing valuable clues about your soul's mission.

Embrace the understanding that the answers you seek lie within you and that you possess an innate capacity to discern your true calling. Release the need for external validation or the influence of societal expectations, and instead, learn to trust the wisdom that emerges from the depths of your being. Nurture a deep sense of self-trust, knowing your inner wisdom guides your journey toward purpose and fulfillment.

You embark on a transformative journey of self-discovery and soul alignment by attuning your attention to the voice of your inner wisdom. This inner compass will illuminate the path that resonates with your authentic self, guiding you toward expressing your unique gifts and contributions. Embrace the power of listening to your inner wisdom as you navigate the twists and turns of your soul's mission, and let it lead you to a life of purpose, fulfillment, and authentic expression.

Cultivate Self-Awareness

Developing a deep understanding of yourself is essential in uncovering your soul's purpose and mission. Cultivate self-awareness through practices such as meditation, journaling, and introspection. These practices allow you to explore your thoughts, emotions, and desires with curiosity and openness.

Take the time to reflect on your values, passions, and what brings you joy and fulfillment. Listen to your intuition and inner guidance as you make decisions and navigate your life's path. Self-awareness helps you identify your strengths, weaknesses, and growth areas, enabling you to align your actions and choices with your authentic self.

Through self-awareness, you gain clarity about who you are and what truly matters to you. This clarity serves as a compass guiding you toward your soul's purpose. It helps you make choices that align with your values and passions, leading to a more fulfilling and purposeful life. Embrace the practice of self-awareness as a powerful tool for self-discovery and finding your unique place in the world.

Reflect Deeply on Your Story and Find Key Patterns and Threads

Engaging in deep reflection on your life story is a crucial step in discovering your soul's purpose. Take the time to look back on your experiences, both positive and challenging, and explore the patterns and threads that have shaped your journey. Examine the recurring themes, lessons, and growth opportunities that have emerged throughout your life.

As you reflect on your story, pay close attention to the moments of struggle and the challenges you have faced. These difficulties often contain valuable insights and lessons to guide you toward your purpose. Look for patterns in your challenges and how you have overcome them. Notice the skills, strengths, and qualities that have helped you navigate those challenges, as they can provide clues about your unique gifts and the contributions you are meant to make.

By examining the patterns and threads of your life, you can gain a deeper understanding of your authentic self and the experiences that have shaped you. This reflection allows you to uncover your core values, passions, and motivations. It reveals how your journey aligns with the world's needs, opening new possibilities for fulfilling your soul's mission. Begin to recognize the strength of your resilience by working through the struggles and the lessons emerging from those challenges. Embrace the transformative power of self-reflection and let it guide you toward a purpose-driven life.

Unearth Your Inherent Gifts and Follow Your Genius

I've found this to be one of the most profound and transformative aspects of discovering purpose and the soul's mission. It's a process of self-exploration and self-discovery that involves delving into the depths of your being to identify the unique talents, strengths, and passions encoded within you. By connecting with your authentic essence and listening to the whispers of your soul, you can uncover the gifts meant to be shared with the world.

Following your genius means honoring and nurturing these gifts, allowing them to guide you toward fulfillment and contribution. It requires aligning your actions, choices, and pursuits with your innate talents and passions rather than following external expectations or societal norms. When you follow your genius, you enter a space of authenticity and alignment where your unique qualities can shine brightly and positively impact the world.

By unearthing your inherent gifts and following your genius, you not only find personal fulfillment but also become a catalyst for inspiration and transformation in the lives of others. As you embrace and cultivate your unique talents, you inspire those around you to do the same. Your authentic expression of self invites others to tap into their own gifts and passions, creating a ripple effect of positive change and empowerment.

You contribute to a greater collective awakening when you align with your genius and embody your soul's mission. Your authentic presence and unique contributions add richness and diversity to the tapestry of human experience. By expressing your gifts, you inspire others to explore their

passions and talents, fostering a culture of authenticity, fulfillment, and purpose.

Be Free to Experiment and Pay Attention to the Doors that Open

Adopting an attitude of openness and experimentation is
essential when discovering your soul's purpose. Recognize
the path may not be linear or clear cut and require exploration and trial and error. Be willing to step outside your
comfort zone, try new things, and embrace the unknown.

Allow yourself to experiment with ideas, activities, and
pursuits that resonate with your heart and soul. Follow your
curiosity and intuition and pay close attention to the doors
that open along the way. The universe often sends signs and
synchronicities to guide you toward your purpose. These
signs can manifest as serendipitous encounters, unexpected opportunities, or positive responses from the world
around you.

By remaining open and attentive to the doors that open
effortlessly and seamlessly, you allow yourself to flow with
the natural rhythm of the universe. Trust these doors are
leading you closer to your soul's mission. Be mindful of the
signs and messages that arise and be willing to adjust your
course or explore new avenues based on the feedback you
receive. Embrace the discovery process and allow yourself
to be guided by the unseen forces conspiring to support
your journey.

Embrace Vulnerability and Take Risks

Discovering your soul's purpose often requires stepping outside your comfort zone and embracing vulnerability. It's about being willing to take risks and explore new territories, even if it means facing uncertainties and challenges along the way. Embracing vulnerability means allowing yourself to be seen, heard, and known in your authentic expression without fearing judgment or rejection.

By embracing vulnerability, you open yourself to new possibilities, opportunities, and growth. Taking risks and pushing beyond your perceived limits allows you to discover hidden talents, passions, and insights about yourself. Embracing vulnerability also cultivates resilience and strengthens your ability to navigate through setbacks and obstacles that may arise on your journey. It allows you to connect deeper with your true self and align your actions with your soul's calling.

As you discover your soul's purpose, remember vulnerability and risk-taking are integral parts of the process. Embrace the discomfort that comes with stepping into the unknown and trust that it is through these courageous acts that you can uncover the profound gifts and potential that lie within you. Allow vulnerability to guide you as you take leaps of faith, challenge self-imposed limitations, and unlock new dimensions of personal growth and fulfillment.

Align with Your Values and Higher Principles

Clarify your core values and the principles that guide your life. Align your actions and choices with these values, ensuring your pursuits are in harmony with your authentic self. When your activities are aligned with your values, you will experience a sense of integrity and fulfillment in your endeavors.

Finding your soul's purpose often involves making a positive impact on others and contributing to something greater than yourself. Explore how your unique gifts and talents can be used to serve others and make a difference in the world. Engage in acts of kindness, volunteer work, or projects that align with your values and allow you to bring your purpose to life.

Remember to Play and Have Fun on the Journey

As you walk the path of soul-searching and deep introspection, it's important to remember that the journey of discovering your soul's purpose is also meant to be joyful and playful. Engage in activities that bring you joy, ignite your creativity, and make you come alive. Explore hobbies, interests, and passions that allow you to express yourself and experience playfulness freely.

When you approach your quest for purpose with a light-hearted and playful attitude, you create space for spontaneity, inspiration, and serendipitous discoveries. Playing and having fun reconnects you with your inner child, allowing you to access a state of wonder, curiosity, and imagination. It opens possibilities, breaks down barriers, and invites new perspectives.

Embrace the spirit of play and allow it to infuse your exploration of purpose with a sense of adventure, curiosity, and delight. Release any attachment to outcomes, engage in activities that please you, and allow your spirit to soar. By cultivating a playful mindset, you invite spontaneity, flexibility, and a sense of lightheartedness into your journey of self-discovery. Remember that play is essential to your soul's mission and vital to living a fulfilling and joyful life.

As you think about your journey, I ask you to consider the following:

- What is your initial reaction to this idea of discovering your soul's mission?
- In what ways have you already been called to your soul's mission on your life journey?
- What challenges and success offer insight into the patterns of your life that speak to your soul's calling?
- What is your understanding of your soul's mission today?
- What are you curious to explore further to discover your soul's mission?

Discovering your soul's mission is a sacred and transformative process that requires deep self-reflection, self-awareness, and alignment with your authentic self. It is a lifelong endeavor to listen to your inner wisdom, embrace vulnerability, and follow your genius. As you cultivate self-awareness, reflect on your story, and unearth your inherent gifts, you align with a greater purpose and make a meaningful impact in the world. You create a life of purpose and fulfillment by embracing vulnerability, taking risks, and aligning with your values and higher principles. Remember to approach this journey with playfulness and joy, allowing your spirit to soar and inviting serendipitous discoveries. Trust in the wisdom that emerges within you and embraces the transformative power of discovering and living your soul's mission.

CHAPTER 14

LEAD WITH WARRIOR COMPASSION

―――

Imagine, if you will, a world in which we come into our fully integrated selves, seeing each other in our full humanity and possessing deeper compassion for ourselves and everyone around us. Consider what this would do to our relationships, workplaces, governments, and society when we begin reimagining systems, structures, and cultures from a place of deeper compassion.

Let's face it: systems are crumbling around us that need to be reimagined, not just rebuilt, through a lens that balances deeper consciousness, compassion, and connection. As we reimagine an emerging future, men engaged in personal development work are essential to bringing about compassion, healing, transformation, and bridge-building worldwide. This work is vital to compassionately build bridges across differences, reframing leadership models, shifting power dynamics, and reimagining systems and structures that transform cultures.

In *Awakening Compassion at Work*, Dr. Monica Worline and Jane Dutton argue compassion is a personal virtue and a fundamental quality that can transform organizational cultures, enhance employee well-being, and improve overall performance. They highlight the importance of creating environments where compassion can thrive, as it has the potential to positively impact employee engagement, collaboration, creativity, and resilience. They also explore the connection between compassion and organizational outcomes such as productivity, employee satisfaction, and customer loyalty (Worline and Dutton 2017).

Before we can transform our world, we must understand this vision will require us to walk an integrated journey into our wholeness and deeper humanity. This can be frightening, as it asks us to be courageous, look at the shadow side of our being, and embrace our wholeness with a deep sense of self-compassion.

Lead with Warrior Compassion

The foundational premise of leading with warrior compassion is integrating strength and empathy in leadership. It recognizes that true leadership requires both the qualities of a warrior, such as courage, resilience, and determination, and the qualities of compassion, including empathy, kindness, and understanding.

Leading with warrior compassion acknowledges that leadership is not solely about achieving goals and results but also about fostering human connection, supporting the growth and well-being of individuals, and creating a positive impact on the world. It recognizes that leaders have the power to influence and inspire others, and with that power comes the responsibility to lead with integrity, empathy, and a genuine concern for the welfare of others.

Warrior compassion emphasizes the importance of standing for what is right and just, advocating for the marginalized or disadvantaged, and confronting challenges and obstacles with unwavering determination. At the same time, it recognizes the significance of approaching these actions with empathy and understanding, considering the needs and perspectives of others, and cultivating a compassionate presence in interactions and decision-making.

The premise of leading with warrior compassion rests on the belief that strength and compassion are not mutually exclusive but complementary qualities that can amplify the effectiveness and impact of leadership. It emphasizes the power of vulnerability, emotional intelligence, and genuine connection in building trust, fostering collaboration, and inspiring others to reach their full potential.

This deepened sense of compassion opens the door to bridge-building conversations where we can overcome differences and elevate traditionally voiceless voices. We can then innovate differently by bringing new and diverse voices into the conversation, which becomes the platform for transforming systems, structures, and cultures in more conscious, compassionate, and connected ways. Ultimately helping teams and organizations perform more seamlessly, innovate more expansively to solve problems differently, and create a more meaningful impact.

Warrior Compassion Leadership Qualities

Leading with warrior compassion is a transformative approach to leadership that combines strength, courage, and empathy. It recognizes that leadership is not just about achieving goals and results, but also about uplifting and empowering others, fostering deep connections, and creating a more compassionate and just world. Leaders who embody warrior compassion lead with their hearts, demonstrating deep compassion, fearlessness in vulnerability, and courageous authenticity. Leading with warrior compassion is a call to embody the qualities of a warrior with the guiding light of compassion, making a profound impact on individuals, organizations, and society. The following are qualities of leaders who lead with warrior compassion:

- **Deep Compassion**
  These leaders have a profound compassion that extends to themselves and others. They approach leadership with empathy, kindness, and understanding and genuinely care about the well-being and growth of those they lead.

- **Fearlessness in Vulnerability**
  These leaders demonstrate courage by embracing vulnerability. They are unafraid to show their authentic selves and share their own struggles and challenges. Being vulnerable creates a safe space for others to do the same, fostering deeper connections and trust.

- **Courageous Authenticity**
  Leaders who lead with warrior compassion show up authentically in all aspects of their leadership. They lead

with integrity and align their actions with their values and beliefs. Their authenticity inspires trust and encourages others to be true to themselves.

- **Radical Self-Compassion**
  Leaders leading with warrior compassion display radical self-compassion. They courageously prioritize their own well-being and self-care, recognizing they can better serve others by taking care of themselves. They set boundaries, practice self-reflection, and prioritize their physical, mental, and emotional health.

- **Resolves Inner Conflicts**
  Leading with warrior compassion, leaders engage in inner work to resolve their own inner conflicts and cultivate harmony within themselves. They are aware of their own biases, triggers, and blind spots, and they continually strive for personal growth and self-improvement.

- **Bold Empathy**
  These leaders exhibit bold empathy, stepping outside their comfort zones to understand and relate to others' experiences and perspectives. They seek to bridge divides and cultivate compassion across differences, even in the face of resistance or discomfort.

- **Bridge Builders**
  These leaders excel in building bridges across differences and fostering inclusivity. They seek to understand diverse perspectives and unite people to find common ground. They create dialogue, respect, and collaborative spaces, enabling individuals to feel seen, heard, and valued.

- **Audacious Advocacy**

  Leaders with warrior compassion boldly advocate for those who have been marginalized or voiceless. They use their positions of influence to speak up against injustice and inequality, championing the rights and well-being of others. They fearlessly challenge systems and structures that perpetuate harm and work toward a more equitable society.

- **Visionary Leadership**

  These leaders have a clear vision for a better future and are driven by a higher purpose. They inspire and motivate others with their vision, rallying people around a shared goal. They foster innovation, creativity, and forward thinking to drive positive change.

- **Trailblazing Innovation**

  These leaders have the courage to innovate and disrupt outdated systems and practices. They challenge conventional wisdom and embrace new ideas and approaches that align with their compassionate vision. They fearlessly lead their teams toward innovative solutions, pushing boundaries and inspiring creativity.

To address the challenges of our times and lead with warrior compassion, leaders need to play three critical roles: emergent facilitator, compassionate bridge builder, and changemaker.

Leader as Emergent Facilitator

Based on my twenty-five years of experience developing leaders and changemakers through facilitation practice, this role is one of the most important for a leader. How a leader holds space and guides others from their deeper intuition is critical to navigating in uncertain times with increasingly complex challenges without clear black-and-white answers.

I've created the Sympónia Method as a leading-edge model transforming leaders through a multimodal facilitation approach. Drawing on various tools, techniques, and strategies, the Sympónia Method empowers and strengthens leaders as emergent facilitators, bridge builders, and changemakers equipped to navigate complex and uncertain challenges and create meaningful global impact.

It emphasizes adaptability, creativity, authenticity, empathy, and collaboration, and it is designed to be flexible and responsive to the unique realities of an evolving world. At its core, this approach helps leaders discover their truth in new ways, understand their core purpose or mission, and learn to trust their inner knowing as they navigate the unknown.

By utilizing the Sympónia Method, leaders can become more impactful agents of change and transformation in their communities and organizations.

The Sympónia Method integrates six facilitation modalities into one model to provide leaders with the skill and agility to hold space and lead transformation in new ways. The six modalities include:

- **Emergent:** A dynamic process of guiding and supporting group interaction that allows new ideas, solutions, and outcomes to emerge from the group's collective wisdom.

- **Transformative:** An intentional process of empowering individuals and groups to create meaningful change through personal growth, increased awareness, and collective action.

- **Systems thinking:** A process of guiding group interactions that encourage participants to consider the relationships, dynamics, and patterns within complex systems.

- **Somatic/embodied:** A body-centered approach to guiding group interactions that integrates physical sensations, movement, and awareness to promote embodied transformation.

- **Contemplative/soulful:** A mindful and reflective approach to guiding group interactions that cultivate inner awareness, deep listening, and connection to the present moment.

- **Creative:** An innovative approach to guiding group interactions that leverage imagination, playfulness, and non-traditional techniques to unlock creativity and generate new ideas.

The Sympónia Method transforms leadership through an intuitive-driven facilitation approach that values collaboration, creativity, and authenticity in individuals, teams, and organizations. This model is grounded in complexity science, systems thinking, design thinking and creativity, and contemplative/embodied practices and aims to create emergent experiences that promote personal and collective growth.

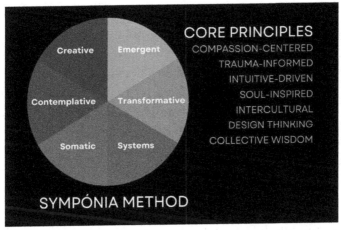

(Image: Harvey 2023)

The Sympónia Method emphasizes the following core principles as a transformative leadership approach:

- **Compassion-centered:** The Sympónia Method is grounded in compassion, placing empathy, kindness, and understanding at the core of its approach. It fosters a nurturing and supportive environment where individuals feel seen, heard, and valued. Compassion-centered practices are integrated throughout facilitation and leadership development, promoting the well-being and growth of all participants.

- **Trauma-informed:** The Sympónia Method acknowledges the impact of trauma on individuals and groups, creating a safe and inclusive space for healing and growth. It incorporates trauma-informed principles, such as recognizing triggers, practicing self-care, and promoting resilience. By understanding the signs and symptoms of trauma, the Sympónia Method empowers individuals to navigate their healing journeys with compassion and sensitivity.

- **Intuitive-driven:** The Sympónia Method embraces intuition as a powerful tool for facilitation and leadership development. It recognizes intuitive guidance can provide valuable insights and directions in decision-making and problem-solving processes. Facilitators and participants can co-create meaningful and impactful experiences that align with their deepest values and intentions by tapping into their inner wisdom.

- **Intercultural:** The Sympónia Method celebrates diversity and promotes intercultural awareness. It values and respects different cultural perspectives, experiences, and backgrounds, fostering an environment of inclusivity and collaboration. By embracing intercultural understanding, the Sympónia Method encourages participants to learn from each other's unique insights and collectively create enriched and comprehensive solutions.

- **Soul-inspired:** The Sympónia Method draws inspiration from the depths of the soul, honoring everyone's unique essence and purpose. It incorporates practices encouraging self-reflection, introspection, and connection with one's authentic self. By tapping into the soul's wisdom and guidance, participants can access their innate creativity, passion, and inner strength, leading to transformative personal and collective growth.

- **Design thinking:** The Sympónia Method applies design thinking principles to facilitation and leadership development. It encourages creative and innovative approaches to problem-solving and decision-making. By embracing an iterative design process, participants can generate new ideas, test them, and refine them based on feedback and reflection. Design thinking fosters a culture of continuous improvement and adaptability.

- **Collective wisdom:** The Sympónia Method harnesses the collective wisdom of the group. It acknowledges that diverse perspectives, experiences, and knowledge enhance problem-solving and decision-making processes. By tapping into collective intelligence, participants can co-create innovative and impactful outcomes that benefit the entire group. The Sympónia Method values collective wisdom as a powerful resource for growth and transformation.

Leader as Compassionate Bridge Builder

When discussing ways to build compassionate bridges across divisions and differences, I notice we often intellectualize or idealize this idea of compassion. However, the real work is to practice and embody compassion in every interaction—visceral, not intellectual—meaning we need to feel it.

I challenge each person I meet by asking how they show unconditional love and compassion to their greatest adversary (the person who hurt them, minimized them, betrayed them, or broke their heart). I then ask how they show unconditional love and compassion to themselves daily. Compassion is action and practice. It's a muscle we must develop, like going to the gym regularly.

This deepened sense of compassion opens the door to bridge-building conversations in which we can overcome differences and elevate traditionally voiceless voices. We can then innovate differently by bringing new and diverse voices into the conversation, which becomes the platform for transforming systems, structures, and cultures in more conscious, compassionate, and connected ways. Ultimately, we can help teams and organizations perform more seamlessly, innovate more expansively to solve problems differently and create a more meaningful impact.

Being a compassionate bridge builder today means actively fostering understanding, connection, and collaboration among individuals, groups, or communities. It involves embodying empathy, openness, and a willingness to bridge divides and overcome barriers to create a more inclusive and harmonious society.

As a compassionate bridge builder, you strive to listen deeply, seeking to understand different perspectives and experiences without judgment. You prioritize empathy and compassion, recognizing every individual's inherent dignity and worth. You engage in respectful dialogue, encouraging open communication and creating spaces for diverse voices to be heard and valued.

Compassionate bridge builders actively work to dismantle systemic barriers and promote equality, justice, and equity. They challenge prejudice, discrimination, and inequality, advocating for social change and fostering environments that embrace diversity and inclusion. They recognize the interconnectedness of all beings and are committed to building bridges across different identities, cultures, and backgrounds.

Being a compassionate bridge builder also requires self-awareness and personal growth. It involves continuously examining one's biases and conditioning and being willing to learn and unlearn to cultivate a deeper understanding of others. It means engaging in ongoing self-reflection, self-care, and self-compassion to sustain and nurture one-self in bridge-building.

Ultimately, being a compassionate bridge builder today means actively contributing to the collective well-being of humanity. It is about fostering connections, building understanding, and working toward a more humane, just, and harmonious world.

Leader as Changemaker

As a change agent and change management professor, I've noticed a lack of empathy and compassion in many organizations, among leaders, and within teams. Now imagine if organizations could support this type of transformation for all employees.

Let's face it: we live in a fractured, out-of-balance world where most institutions and systems have been built around a traditional masculine model—one that doesn't typically allow for genuine authenticity, full emotional expression, and deep connection. It's not that the masculine models are bad or wrong, but they are incomplete. Based on how systems have been designed and developed, most of these systems, structures, cultures, and institutions have been built on a masculine ideal that favors men and the masculine.

As we think about the evolution of leadership and power dynamics, the models shift from fear-based control to love-based empowerment. At management conferences, more experts are talking about conscious leadership; the ideas of love, compassion, and deeper humanity are being introduced into more organizational systems with greater acceptance.

This is often introduced as human-centered workplace design or conscious/compassionate leadership.

As change makers, leaders have the capacity to develop compassion-centered systems change models that support these human-centered approaches. Consider the impact of the evolution from fear-based control to love-based liberation on our organizational systems, structures, and cultures. This organizational transformation begins with leaders engaging in healing and personal transformation work that will evolve how they view and lead organizations.

The evolution is happening so quickly that by the time you read this book, a dozen new concepts for transforming leadership, systems, and cultures could exist. Ultimately, organizations will be designed to be more conscious, compassionate, and connected through human-centered approaches.

Evolving Our Collective Consciousness

I've had many experiences recently that have demonstrated a shift happening in organizational systems. I had a conversation with someone from a global bank who asked if I could help change agents and learning specialists in the company become more vulnerable to allow more vulnerability in facilitated spaces for the employees and leaders. A police chief also asked me if I could help deepen the level of compassion among new officers and to hold space for conversations among officers and the community to humanize each other and develop a new relationship in the future. A defense missiles contractor once asked me if I could give a talk on compassion through a military voice so the engineers could create a more compassionate culture.

As we talk about transforming leadership models, systems, and cultures, we must start using different language and approaches from what's out there now. Frankly, much of what's out there today just isn't working. We are more divided than ever, and people seem to be unwilling to budge on their point of view and perspective. We're talking at and about each other, but I don't see as much talking with each other.

As we begin to talk with each other from a place of curiosity, compassion, and love, we can start building compassionate bridges across our divisions and differences. What if we invited each other into the conversations rather than demanding that the other side get our point of view? By unearthing our truth, we see the truth and humanity in someone else, and even if we don't agree, we get curious to understand and accept each other's truth. What would be possible?

As the systems around us continue to crumble, we can see problems that need to be fixed or wounds that need to be healed. And many people are confused and feeling lost; this is where compassion comes in rather than rightness, righteousness, and judgment. Compassion is the antidote to judgment where we have choices—fear or love, scarcity or abundance, fixing or healing. Compassion is what is most needed now, more than anything.

Warrior compassion can ignite a global compassionate healing movement with its courageous and loving energy. As men tap into their inner warrior and embark on their healing journeys, they become catalysts for transformation, inspiring others to face their wounds and limitations. This movement extends beyond personal growth, permeating societal structures and systems, advocating for well-being and justice for all. It fosters a world where compassion guides decision-making, policy development, and human interactions, creating an interconnected and healed world where the liberation of the individual is intertwined with the liberation of all.

As you think about your journey, I ask you to consider the following:

- What does it mean to lead with warrior compassion?
- What leadership qualities do you embody, and what qualities do you aspire to develop?
- What becomes possible when we shift from fear-based control to love-based liberation in our systems?
- How will organizations look different when cultures are more conscious, compassionate, and connected?
- How can healing warriors support the development of these cultures?

Embracing the path of leading with warrior compassion can transform our world on individual, organizational, and societal levels. By delving into our own healing and integration, we can cultivate a deep sense of self-compassion and tap into the power of love and empathy. By embodying compassionate leadership, we can drive innovative systems change and foster a culture of connection, inclusivity, and well-being. As we navigate the complexities of our world, let us remember compassion is not a sign of weakness but a powerful force for transformation and collective growth.

The Sympónia Method provides a comprehensive framework for leaders to facilitate meaningful change, while compassionate bridge-building and changemaking allow us to create more inclusive and harmonious environments. By embracing compassionate masculinity and nurturing cultures grounded in empathy and connection, we can bring about transformative systems change and culture transformation.

As compassionate bridge builders, we can foster understanding, connection, and collaboration, bridging divides and creating inclusive environments. We can challenge existing systems and cultures by embracing changemaker roles and ushering in a new era of conscious, compassionate, and connected leadership. Through the synergy of personal transformation and systemic change, we can co-create a more compassionate, just, and harmonious world for all. Let us embark on this transformative journey with courage, empathy, and a deep commitment to the power of warrior compassion.

CHAPTER 15

UNLEASH YOUR HEALING POWER IN THE WORLD

As we reach the final chapter of *Warrior Compassion*, it is an opportune time to reflect on our profound journey together. We have explored the depths of compassion-centered leadership, soul healing, and the transformative power of love. We dove into self-discovery, personal growth, and societal change. As we conclude this remarkable odyssey, we find ourselves standing at the threshold of a new world rooted in compassion, interconnectedness, and the integration of our deepest selves.

Throughout these pages, we have embraced the wisdom and teachings of visionary leaders, scholars, and spiritual traditions. We have explored the writings of individuals who have dedicated their lives to soul mission, compassionate leadership, and healing our collective wounds. We have witnessed the transformative power of self-compassion and its ripple effects on our relationships, organizations, and the world at large.

The essence of our journey can be distilled into a profound realization: compassion is the key that unlocks the door to our shared humanity. The thread weaves us together, dissolving the illusions of separation and allowing us to embrace our interconnectedness. When we approach ourselves and others with compassion, we transcend the limitations of fear, judgment, and division. We create a space where healing can occur, wounds can be transformed into sources of strength, and love can flourish.

Compassion is not a passive sentiment or a fleeting emotion; it is an active force that calls us to action. It requires us to extend a helping hand, listen deeply, and hold space for one another's pain and joy. It asks us to see beyond the surface, recognize the inherent worth and dignity of every being, and strive for justice, equity, and inclusivity. Compassion challenges us to step outside our comfort zones and advocate and give voice to the voiceless.

Our journey has also revealed the power of personal transformation as a catalyst for societal change. As we engage in our healing work, we become vessels of compassion, radiating love and understanding into the world. Our healing journeys intertwine with the collective, creating a tapestry of open-heartedness that has the potential to reshape our systems, structures, and cultures.

The path of compassionate transformation has its challenges. It requires courage, vulnerability, and a willingness to confront our shadows. It calls us to question the status quo, challenge oppressive systems, and dismantle the walls that separate us. However, in the face of these challenges, we find strength, resilience, and a deep sense of purpose.

As we embrace the fullness of our humanity and awaken to the truth of our interconnectedness, we become agents of change, catalysts for a more compassionate and just world. Our voices merge with the chorus of healing warriors dedicated to creating a global healing movement that transcends boundaries, cultures, and generations.

We will begin to find each other based on our shared energetic resonance. As we follow our soul's mission, each of us, through our gifts and genius, holds a piece to a larger puzzle that nobody can see alone but will understand how the pieces fit when we join in community.

Together, we reimagine our organizations, institutions, and societies from a place of deeper consciousness, compassion, and connection. We bridge the divides that separate us and create spaces where diverse voices are heard, valued, and empowered. We infuse our leadership models with empathy, kindness, and love, nurturing environments in which individuals can thrive and contribute their unique gifts to the world. We will inject a more profound sense of humanity into our systems and institutions to help us evolve as a society.

At the root of this global compassionate healing movement is the transforming power of love. As I worked backward from this vision, I realized that helping men heal, love, and connect on a deeper level was the critical lever point to the larger vision of systems change. When each man transforms into the truth of who he is, begins to love the truth of who he is, realizes his gifts, hears the call of his soul, understands his purpose, and courageously carries out his mission, he will evolve into his sacred masculine and bring about an energetic resonance that has the power to bring healing into the world.

As more men engage in this work at the soul level, we create a collective energetic resonance that forms the global healing movement of compassionate healing that will transform our world. This movement extends beyond personal growth, permeating societal structures and systems, advocating for well-being and justice for all. It fosters a world where compassion guides decision-making, policy development, and human interactions, creating an interconnected and healed world where the liberation of the individual is intertwined with the liberation of all.

As we conclude this journey, let us carry the flame of *Warrior Compassion* within our hearts and minds. Let us be guided by the wisdom we have gained, the lessons we have learned, and the transformations we have experienced. Let us embody compassionate leadership daily, extending kindness and understanding to ourselves and all those we encounter. May compassionate healing and transformation continue to unfold, illuminating our path and inspiring future generations.

As you think about your journey, I ask you to consider the following:

- What are you taking from this journey over the last fifteen chapters?
- How are you being called to contribute to the world?
- What healing work do you want to explore further?
- What impact do you hope to make in the world?
- What are your next steps in your healing journey?
- What are your next steps as a healing warrior?

The journey of men unleashing their healing power in the world is a profound and transformative path. It begins with the recognition that personal healing and self-compassion are essential for our own well-being and the collective healing of humanity. As we embark on this journey, we discover the interconnectedness of our own healing with the transformation of systems, structures, and cultures.

Let us embrace the transformative power within us and honor the journey of healing and compassion. As we continue to walk this path together, we can reshape our world, heal its wounds, and create a brighter future for all. May unconditional love guide our actions, and may compassion be the driving force that brings us closer to the world we envision.

ACKNOWLEDGMENTS

——

I want to thank my Divine Creator for giving me the experiences, intuitive hits, courage, and strength to walk this path and for the insights and wisdom shared throughout this book.

I also want to take this moment to thank my family and friends who have been my champions, my cheerleaders, my co-conspirators, and my challengers throughout my life who have inspired the stories in this book.

I want to thank the men of the Harvey clan, especially my father and grandfather and my Cherokee ancestors, who have sacrificed so much for me to have this opportunity to share my insights and wisdom with other men.

And finally, to my mom, Sue Weddell, and all the women who have been guides, healers, and teachers to help me come into my integration, balance, and healing as a man to carry out my mission.

A special shoutout to my Soulful Facilitators and Compassionate Bridge Builders for offering continued support and love at every step of this writing journey.

And a thank you to all of the men whom I've met or spoken to who have inspired the messages and kernels of insight and wisdom throughout the pages of this book.

I also want to thank all of those who were interviewed for this book:

Brian Anderson, Ray Arata, Joseph Bernstein, Abriana Bernstein, William Broniec, Jennifer Brown, Marcelo Cardoso, Perry Carrison, Julien Chaix, Michael Chamberlain, Walter Crawford, Jed Diamond, Quentin Finney, Ed Frauenheim, Ludo Gabrielle, Conya Gilmore, Lion Goodman, Ross Guttler, Boysen Hodgson, Monroe Howard, Fabienne Jacquet, Aaron Kahlow, Gabriel Keczan, Al Klein, James Kress, Marshall Kupka-Moore, Joe Laur, Owen Marcus, Brian McComak, Soma Miller, Nick Montoya, Ken Mossman, Brandon Peele, Antuan Raimone, Valerie Rivera, Ankara Rose, Martin Rutte, John Scilipote, Mike Shereck, Barney Singer, Jake Stitka, Travis Scott, Charles Sue-Wah-Sing, Eric Thomas, Glenn Thomas, Christopher Veal, Heather Wagner, and James Young.

And a special thank you to all of my early backers who supported me by pre-ordering a copy of *Warrior Compassion:*

Stephen Aguirre, Tamu Al-Islam, Ellema Albert Neal, Brian Anderson, Phil Andrew, Emily Aldredge, Erika Allison, Carol Asiagh, Maria Badali, Robert Beaven, Matteo Becchi,

Abriana Bernstein, Joseph Bernstein, Bonnie Betters, Monica Biggs, Jana Bilski, Shelby Blake, Karen Bona, Shari Brink, William Broniec, Maria Buda, Anne Burke Piotrzkowski, Jayne Burke, Marcelo Cardoso, Perry Carrison, Daniel Chappell, Suzy Clausen, Andrew Cohn, Susan Coleman, Christin Collins, Anahka Coman, Alise Cortez, Walter Crawford, Tony Cruise, Susan Crumiller, Duncan Cryle, MaryAnn D'Ambrosio, Barb Danielewski, Dennis Deany, Cameron DeBerry, Heidi Dewan, Lisa Dolce, Jeff Fanselow, Jeremy Fernandes-Fontana, Quentin Finney, Ed Frauenheim, Judith Gail, Rick Gage, Gail Garland, Matthew Gayton, Jerri Goldberg, Andrew Gordon-Kirsch, Mark Greene, Linda Guttler, Ross Guttler, Amy Hall, Michael Harrigan, Patty Heilman, Nick Hodulik, Matthew Hogan, Boysen Hodgson, Marcia Hyatt, Jill Hyland, Shana James, Yvette Jarreau, Katherine Johnson, Cheryl Lynn Jones, Aaron Kahlow, Diana Karczmarczyk, Jared Karol, Ron Karstetter, John Kelly, Allison King, Andrew Kippen, Eric Koester, Patrick Kozakiewicz, James Kress, Jade Ku, Marshall Kupka-Moore, Joe Laranjeiro, Catherine Lada, Dominic Longo, Mary Luke, Brian Madigan, Anna Mak, David Marcus, Cindy Malm, Brian McComak, Rosalba Messina, Angela Migliaccio, Brian Monthe, Jana Mitzoda, Cindy Morgan-Olson, Ken Mossman, Judi Neal, Michael Nila, Suzanne O'Connor, Michael Ovadia, Sarah Owen, Steve Parris, Christian Pelkonen, Peter Prichard, David Purdy, Antuan Raimone, Nicole Rattless, Elizabeth Richardson, Lisa Ripley Becker, Leslie Ritter, Elana Roberts, Nico Rosenstone, John Ruhl, John Scilipote, Kyla Shawyer, Aaron Shneyer, Karen Shiel, Andrew Snavely, Michael Steiner, Travis Stock, Jason Teeters, Michael Tennant, Glenn Thomas, Robert Torres, Edward Trout, Tomomi Uetani, Christopher Veal, Christopher Vega, Heather Wagner, Muriel Watkins,

Susan Weddell, Samuel Weeks, Mikel Welch, Michael Welp, Dena Wiggins, Pattie Williams, Scott Williams, James Young, and Jill Zinckgraf.

A special thank you to my beta readers who offered fresh perspectives on the book: Tamu al-Islam, Brian Anderson, Amanda Buschi, Jeff Fanselow, and Jim Rhoads.

And finally, to my dear friends whom I spoke with almost daily who kept me going, talked me off the ledge when I wanted to quit, and helped me keep my sanity over the last couple of years of this crazy journey: Heather Wagner, Leslie Ritter, Dena Wiggins, Patty Heilman, Tamu Al-Islam, Quentin Finney, Jeff Fanselow, and Jason Teeters.

APPENDIX

Introduction

Safire, William. 1997. "Keeping Your Powder Dry," *New York Times*, February 23, 1997. https://www.nytimes.com/1997/02/23/magazine/keeping-your-powder-dry.html.

Chapter 1: The Plight of the Wounded Warrior

CDC (Centers for Disease Control and Prevention). n.d. "About Multiple Cause of Death, 2018-2021, Single Race." Accessed June 27, 2022. http://wonder.cdc.gov/mcd-icd10-expanded.html.

Cigna Group. 2023. "The Loneliness Epidemic Persists: A Post-Pandemic Look at the State of Loneliness among US Adults." Accessed June 19, 2023. https://newsroom.thecignagroup.com/loneliness-epidemic-persists-post-pandemic-look.

Cox, Daniel. 2021. "The State of American Friendship: Change, Challenges, and Loss." Survey Center on American Life. June 8, 2021. https://www.americansurveycenter.org/research/the-state-of-american-friendship-change-challenges-and-loss.

Equimundo: Center for Masculinities and Social Justice. 2023. *State of American Men 2023: From Crisis and Confusion to Hope*. Accessed May 23, 2023. https://www.equimundo.org/wp-content/uploads/2023/05/State-of-American-Men-2023.pdf.

Murthy, Vivek. 2023. *Our Epidemic of Loneliness and Isolation: The US Surgeon General's Advisory on the Healing Effects of Social Connection and Community*. US Department of Health and Human Services. Accessed June 1, 2023. https://www.hhs.gov/sites/default/files/surgeon-general-social-connection-advisory.pdf.

NIMH (National Institute for Mental Health). 2022. "Past Year Prevalence of Major Depressive Episode Among US Adults (2020)." Accessed May 15, 2023. https://www.nimh.nih.gov/health/statistics/major-depression.

US Census Bureau. 2022. "Census Bureau Releases New Educational Attainment Data." Accessed May 15, 2023. https://www.census.gov/newsroom/press-releases/2022/educational-attainment.html.

Chapter 2: Warrior Compassion as a Healing Power

Oxford English Dictionary. 2023. "Compassion." accessed June 22, 2023. https://www.oed.com/viewdictionaryentry/Entry/37475.

Adams, Edward and Ed Frauenheim. 2020. *Reinventing Masculinity: The Liberating Power of Compassion and Connection*. Oakland, CA: Barrett-Kohler Publishers, Inc.

Chapter 3: My Healing Journey at EILEEN FISHER

Betters-Reed, Bonnie, Michael Harvey, and Judi Neal. 2020. "Nurturing the Soul of the Company at EILEEN FISHER." *The Jour-

nal of Management, Spirituality, and Religion 17, no. 3 (April):
211. https://www.tandfonline.com/doi/abs/10.1080/14766086.
2020.1752994.

Harvey, Michael. 2019. "Breaking Convention: My Journey as a
Man at EILEEN FISHER." *Wharton Wharton Quarterly* 8, no. 1
(Winter): 35. https://www.whartonhealthcare.org/breaking_
convention_my_journey_as_a_man_at_eileen_fisher_
embracing_and_elevating_the_feminine.

Harvey, Michael. 2020. "The Power of Integrated Leadership."
Wharton Healthcare Quarterly 9, no. 3 (Summer): 32.
https://www.whartonhealthcare.org/the_power_of_integrated_
leadership.

Chapter 4: Embarking on My Soul Adventure

Ingerman, Sandra. 2012. *Shamanic Journeying: A Beginners Guide.*
Surry Hills, New South Wales: ReadHowYouWant.

Palmer, Parker. 2004. *The Hidden Wholeness: The Journey Toward
an Undivided Life—Welcoming the Soul and Weaving Community in a Wounded World.* New York: John Wiley & Sons. Inc.

Chapter 5: Prepare for Your Healing Journey

Brown, Brené. 2012. *The Power of Vulnerability: Teachings of
Authenticity, Connection, and Courage.* Louisville, KY: Sounds
True.

Singer, Michael. 2007. *The Untethered Soul: The Journey Beyond
Yourself.* Oakland, CA: New Harbinger Publications, Inc.

Veal, Christopher. 2022. *The Whole Man: Evolving Masculinity.*
Washington, D.C.: New Degree Press.

Chapter 6: Begin the Journey as an Inquiry

Frankl, V.E. 1963. *Man's Search for Meaning: An Introduction to Logotherapy.* New York: Washington Square Press.

Pollan, Michael. 2019. *How to Change Your Mind: What the New Science of Psychedelics Teaches Us About Consciousness, Dying, Addiction, Depression, and Transcendence.* New York: Penguin Books.

Chapter 7: Deepen Spiritual Understanding

Barks, Coleman. 2004. *The Essential Rumi, New Expanded Edition.* New York: HarperOne.

Dalai Lama. 1998. *The Art of Happiness: A Handbook for Living.* New York: Riverhead Books.

Ingerman, Sandra. 1991. *Soul Retrieval: Mending the Fragmented Self.* San Francisco: HarperOne.

Wilber, Ken. 2007. *Integral Spirituality: A Startling New Role for Religion in the Modern and Postmodern World.* Boulder, CO: Shambhala Publications.

Chapter 8: Unearth the Deeper Wounds

Bly, Robert. 1990. *Iron John: A Book About Men.* Reading, MA: Addison-Wesley.

Diamond, Jed. 2004. *The Irritable Male Syndrome: Understanding and Managing the 4 Key Causes of Depression and Aggression.* Emmaus, PA: Rodale Books.

Ford, Debbie. 2010. *The Dark Side of the Light Chasers: Reclaiming Your Power, Creativity, Brilliance, and Dreams*. New York: Riverhead Books.

Jung, C. G. 1959. Aion: *Researches into the Phenomenology of the Self. Collected Works of C.G. Jung*, Volume 9 (Part 2), 2nd edition. Princeton, NJ: Princeton University Press.

Masters, Robert Augustus. 2018. *To Be a Man: A Guide to True Masculine Power*. Louisville, KY: Sounds True.

Chapter 9: Embrace the Soul-Healing Journey

Schucman, Helen. 1976. *A Course in Miracles: Combined Volume*. Mill Valley, CA: Foundation for Inner Peace.

Chapter 10: Walk the Soul-Healing Path

Fox, Matthew. 2008. *The Hidden Spirituality of Men: Ten Metaphors to Awaken the Sacred Masculine*. Novato, CA: New World Library.

Neff, Kristen. 2015. *Self-Compassion: The Proven Power of Being Kind to Yourself*. New York: William Morrow Paperbacks.

Chapter 11: Expand Your Capacity to Love

hooks, bell. 2004. *The Will to Change: Men, Masculinity, and Love*. New York: Washington Square Press.

Levine, Amir and Rachel Heller. 2012. *Attached: The New Science of Adult Attachment and How It Can Help You Find—and Keep—Love*. New York: TarcherPerigee.

Young, Jim. 2022. *Expansive Intimacy: How Tough Guys Defeat Burnout*. Washington, DC: New Degree Press.

Chapter 12: Emerge as Healing Warriors

Rohr, Richard. 2011. *Falling Upward: A Spirituality for the Two Halves of Life*. New York: Josey-Bass.
Masters, Robert Augustus. 2018. *To Be a Man: A Guide to True Masculine Power*. Louisville, KY: Sounds True.

Chapter 13: Discover Your Soul's Mission

Zukav, Gary. 1989. *The Seat of the Soul*. New York: Simon & Schuster.

Chapter 14: Lead with Warrior Compassion

Worline, Monica and Jane Dutton. 2017. *Awakening Compassion at Work: The Quiet Power that Elevates People and Organizations*. Oakland, CA: Barrett-Kohler Publishers, Inc.

ABOUT THE AUTHOR

—

Sean Harvey, MSOD, MSEd, is an organization development consultant, master facilitator and mentor, professor, TEDx speaker, interfaith minister, and men's soul adventure guide. He received the Saul A. Silverman 2021 Award for Conflict Resolution and Healing from the International Organization Development Association for his healing work with men in hypermasculine systems.

His work in personal, organizational, and societal transformation is inspired by twenty-five years of purpose, leadership, and organization development consulting combined with having served on the faculties of Cornell, New York University, and Baruch College CUNY, teaching courses in the areas of leadership, management, and organizational behavior and change. Sean is affiliated with George Washington University's Center for Excellence in Public Leadership in Washington, DC. He is a co-founder of Project Compassion, a national initiative to deepen compassion in police departments and communities. In 2021, he delivered his TEDx called "Compassion Makes the Warrior." Learn more about his work at www.warriorcompassion.com.

Made in the USA
Middletown, DE
09 September 2023

37941856R00136